CW00427994

SURRENDER

Table of contents

I was now ready for treatment

The excitement of starting the day

So many character defects

Poem – Character defects

Bonding and becoming part of the group

There is no quick fix to rebuild the trust

Poem – Trust

At night before the light goes out

My final day of treatment

All is well, right here, right now

Part 2 – How I stay in recovery on a daily basis

Daily self-care

A set of ingredients

Poem – Desire

Spirituality

Higher Power

Poem – Higher Power

My daily self-care activities

Prayer and meditation

Gratitude

Changing negative thinking to positive

Self-esteem

AA meetings and the fellowship

Endless support

Poem – AA and the fellowship

The 12 steps

Poem – The 12 steps

Daily reflections

Aftercare

Rehabs

Triggers and boundaries

Poem – Triggers

Dealing with relationships

Poem – Dealing with relationships

Comparing yourself to others

Deflection

Complacency

The three stages of a relapse – emotional, mental and physical

Relapse is an opportunity

It is now down to you

Poem – It is now down to you

A final comment for what it's worth

Julian Morgan – author biography

Preface

It was during the first Covid lockdown in the UK in March 2020 that I decided to start writing this book. Like so many others, I spent much of the day channel-hopping on TV, and among other programmes, I found myself watching several documentaries following the incarcerated lives of people in prisons around the world. For me, this became compulsive viewing. There were endless interviews with inmates, and I noticed that there was one question to which most of the answers were identical. This question was asking the prisoners why they were there, and it was their answer that gave me the inspiration to put pen to paper for this book.

It was almost invariably due to their alcohol or drug addiction that they could not stop reoffending. Their crime was essential to them, as it supported their habit. On further questioning, it materialised that nearly every single one of them was totally fed up with this endless cycle, acknowledging they were helpless in the face of their addiction but stating that they had no idea how to stop drinking or using. I could see, hear and feel their desperation, and it certainly was not staged for the camera; these people really and truly had had enough of their current existence and wanted to change their lives. But all too often, they didn't know how.

There are many excellent books that describe emotional stories about disastrous situations and events, and the consequences of addiction on people's lives. All these stories are fundamentally the same, apart from the severity of the problem. But the key point is that addiction is not a choice. Few people choose to become alcoholics or addicts and effectively wreck their own lives. But it happens, and too often, people are plunged into a process far beyond their understanding and their control. Those people I saw on TV needed a simple, straightforward book explaining a process that they could understand and offering hope and freedom from their addictions. Then it occurred to me that there are millions of others around the world from every walk of life who are trying to hide or cover up their addictions and are also longing for the same recovery outcome without being exposed to a badly labelled and unjustified stigma. Despite increasing understanding of mental health and its relation to drug and alcohol problems, our society still tends to have certain stereotyped views of alcoholics and addicts as being 'down and outs' or 'in the gutter', but the truth is that addiction entraps a very wide range of people. It does not matter if you are homeless or a CEO, student or professor, soldier or officer, criminal or barrister – addiction favours no one, and everyone is vulnerable.

My book *Surrender* will outline this process to you and hopefully will give you the help you need for long-term recovery from addiction. Whether you are still drinking or using, in early recovery, or well acquainted with the recovery process, it contains tools and skills that are useful, indeed vital, at any stage of recovery, including relapse. Only one in seven people worldwide suffering from alcohol and drug use disorder receive treatment. I very much hope this book reaches some of them.

I am 56 years of age and was a chronic alcoholic for decades. There were some very early signs of my future alcohol issues even at the age of 10. I was the youngest, having two brothers and sisters, and even then I used to ask to finish the wine dregs from the bottle the family would traditionally have with the Sunday roast. I was also pretty good at tennis, playing in my club's senior first team at the age of 12, and I would frequently win. I was treated as an adult in the 'Après' match social scene, consuming pints on a regular basis and quite often getting drunk.

You would think that the sight of a drunken boy who is not even a teenager might arouse concern in those witnessing it. Not at all. In those days, issues with alcohol were totally ignored. Anyone labelled an alcoholic or drug addict was looked down upon as being the utmost scum of the earth, and there was minimal awareness of alcoholism or addiction. So individuals like myself, when I was slightly older, were seen as barflies, pissheads, booze hounds or young socialites. It was accepted, so any concerns for my future physical dependency and mental obsession weren't even considered.

To gain independence, maturity and experience, at the age of 17 I volunteered to work on a kibbutz and moshav in Israel for eight months. This was where I was introduced to 'top shelf' (spirits with extremely high alcohol content) and would quite easily drink a bottle of the local vodka or a Middle Eastern spirit called Arak, which was rocket fuel. After a short stint of sobriety in the British Army, I became a successful photocopier salesman in London, and due to outrageous commission bonuses, I was able literally to pour alcohol down my throat. The severe recession of the early 1990s enabled me to pack a rucksack and backpack around the southern hemisphere for a year. This subsequently turned into 10 years due to my employment – night club and bar management! I would drink for free and, over time, became physically dependent on alcohol.

So, from drinking a bottle of spirits occasionally in my teens, I was now in my early 30s and drinking a litre a day, sometimes more. This escalation led to my nervous system collapsing in my legs. I could hardly walk, and my mental health was crumbling, too. It was now a choice – to try and find a way to recover, or to pick a nice, cosy coffin.

I made my choice, and gratefully, I have been alcohol free for several years by surrendering to this recovery process, enabling me to have daily sobriety and the freedom to appreciate a life full of love, happiness and joy.

By the way, when I went to look, there weren't any nice cosy coffins available in my preferred shade of oak . . .

Introduction

I have written my recovery process in two halves, with separate styles of writing.

The first half is a profound and sincerely written account of my final stay at a residential drug and alcohol rehabilitation centre. It describes the relentless, confusing struggle with denial, helplessness and dishonesty, the constant pull towards drinking, and my battle for life-saving sobriety. These chapters detail my isolated and purposeless existence that thrived on shame, guilt and fear, highlighting the anxiety and paranoia that infested my emotions, resulting in despair and desperation. These were sensitive and sometimes dramatic times that I would not want to relive.

This is when I discovered spirituality and my Higher Powers – terms that I will explain more further on in the book but that I understand as entities I can trust and have faith in to guide me along a new path, with a direction that allows me to change my life and enjoy daily sobriety. Finally, I had the willingness to surrender to a process that would give me the strength as well as the desire never to drink again.

The second half is a precise, straightforward account of how I stay free of addiction on a daily basis. I have deliberately kept this chronicle simple to read and to follow, with basic explanations and examples, as it is imperative that there is no confusion or misunderstanding. In many ways, staying recovered can be the hardest part of the journey. I compare it to a diet; losing weight is relatively easy, but being able to keep at that weight may prove to be extremely difficult. It can, however, be done, and that is what this half of the book is all about.

This half of the recovery journey includes a set of tasks and tools that I use to create a daily self-care recovery plan that has gratefully kept me sober for a few years now. The process never ceases to give me hope, faith and courage and to keep me from the destructive bondage and imminent death threat of an alcoholic obsession.

I have also written a sequence of poems that relate to various chapters in the recovery journey. Poetry is a highly enjoyable and worthwhile thing that I am fortunate enough to be able to write, after finding this amateur talent in an art therapy class while staying at one of many treatment centres. Writing both poetry and prose can be very therapeutic and is one of the measures I encourage you to try during the course of this book. You could look at your words being lyrics to a favourite song to really express your feelings.

This poetic sequence offers another method of explanation and doubles the impact with a different angle of dramatic emotion. These can also be easier to understand and remember if there are certain areas within the recovery process that some readers are finding tricky and hard to grasp. I use repetition throughout the book on purpose, as I am trying my hardest for everything to stick!! I know from experience that it is beneficial, sometimes needful, for people to hear and read the same message repeatedly, to help the assimilation process.

Writing this book has helped my own recovery immensely by tidying up any loose ends that might have frayed, so I am so grateful to you all who have decided to address your own issues by reading my journey.

Please, open your heart and mind and enjoy what you are about to read, and if one single word, sentence, paragraph or page has helped you on your journey towards addiction recovery, I have achieved what I set out to do.

This book – *Surrender*

This day has taken so long to arrive.

Possibly I have found the answer on how to survive.

Surrender is a book that opens new paths,

An addiction recovery story written in two halves.

Opening locked gates giving a new direction,

Removing the lies, enabling honest reflection.

Years of denial it will totally expose,

Then expelling it to an abyss where no one goes.

It will remove the handcuffs and let you go free,

Introducing a process to read, think and finally see,

Outlining a successful daily self-care plan

Called keeping a clean house where you will become a fan,

With imperative but simple tasks and tools

To keep away the slips that lead to falls.

The importance of gratitude you will find out

As it generates positivity without a doubt.

So now not taking anything for granted,

Finding appreciation from which you will never be parted,

Explaining spirituality to find your Higher Power

For it to grow your recovery from seed to a flower,

Using a set of unique principles called the twelve steps

Which require daily practice and be assured are not complex.

There will be addiction meetings in every town –

AA is my choice to attend and is imperative if I am down.

In this room you will find a sponsor possibly becoming a friend,

Making sure that any rules you do not try and bend,

And showing you the steps for a permanent desire

Not to drink or use, and extinguishing that fatal, insidious fire.

This book must outline the three stages of relapse –

An emotional, mental and physical cycle ending in collapse

But mistakes will happen, so this is a huge opportunity

To start again, recharge the batteries and this time see

That addiction with its lingering obsession

Leading to shame, guilt, worthlessness and depression,

Will be banished for the very last time

Due to your strength and faith, resulting in a feeling so sublime.

Now is the time to open your mind and heart

To produce a magical journey that you will progressively chart.

Enjoy reading and discover freedom within these pages,

Only a short book, mind you, but it took absolutely ages,

You can look afar but my honest story is one of a kind,

As another personal detailed recovery process you will not find,

It does not dwell on a past traumatic horrendous story,

IT IS A TALE OF ADDICTION RECOVERY IN ALL ITS GLORY.

Part 1

How I recovered

I wasn't in denial – I could have easily stopped drinking

Why did I go to rehab? I didn't need to be there. I could have gone a few days without drinking. But then again, did I ever do that? I always thought I could, but was I being honest and realistic? – Blimey. In the beginning, I was so confused and muddled I needed a drink!

My sobriety is what my family wanted, but what did it have to do with them, anyway? It was my life, and I was okay. They had distanced themselves, not even inviting me to family occasions and totally ignoring my calls and texts. When they did phone, why were they so concerned with my addiction, attitude and health? Surely, if they loved me, they would stop mentioning it, stop saying that rehab was my only option, knowing it would upset me? I had told them so many times that I didn't need to go to a place like that and that there are so many people who drink heavily like me. I just did not realise that I was hiding my existence behind a mask, enabling anything that would allow me to drink, thinking that my acute, severe anxiety and panic attacks were due to the normal pressures of everyday life.

My friends thought I should speak to someone. They weren't my real friends, or they would have just left me alone. It was none of their business, and I told them that. My true friends were in the bar chatting and telling stories, and I loved every minute of it, even though the same tales were repeated daily. No one could remember one day from another, so the conversations always seemed interesting and witty. It was sociable, and we all enjoyed each other's company. One thing I couldn't understand, though, was that no one else ever came over from another group to say hello. I put that down to them being arrogant and rude. Never mind the fact that after these sessions I frequently had difficulty getting home. More than once, I even ended up with fractured bones from intoxicated tumbles on the pavement, trying to navigate my way home when the bar had closed. Of course, that was nothing to do with me or my drinking.

I was told that my bones were brittle due to my drinking, and eventually, because of my alcohol abuse, my nervous system short-circuited, significantly affecting the movement of my legs. I struggled to walk and would lose balance for no apparent reason. They say that alcoholism is a progressive disease, or is it a mental illness? I ended up being barred from countries and airlines due to altercations at airports and on flights. Looking back, it is extraordinary that I was never handed a prison sentence in England or abroad for countless such drunken offences. I ran out of money. I had no idea why I lost my last job – well, my last three. In fact, my work regularly ended with me being fired, which seems so unfair as I'm a nice guy and I'm pretty sure I did everything they asked of me. Even my friends in the bar couldn't understand it and bought me a few pints in sympathy. Lovely people saying that there was nothing wrong with me and to just forget about those idiots, as they have no respect for normal people. My girlfriends were the same, very comforting and understanding, with alcohol acting as Cupid to start the relationship – but I could never work out why they didn't last for more than a month . . .

So, in the end, I decided to go into rehab just to keep everyone else happy. I thought it would be a walk in the park, as I would be totally different from all the others. I was always absolutely convinced that I wasn't the problem – it was everyone else, totally misjudging me. I always thought that for some reason they were jealous of my routine and lifestyle and hence wanted to sabotage it for me. My drinking bar buddies agreed.

Denial

Drinking for me has not ever been an issue

And certainly something I would never admit to,

Despite what people say, I can always control it.

It is normal to have blackouts and an alcohol withdrawal fit.

If I was asked to stop for a single day

It would be easy, with no second thought or momentary delay.

It is everyone else who does not understand me –

I am fine, which they are so blind to see.

Yes, I have lost absolutely everything in my life –

My job, my savings, my whole family, including the wife,

But this is not alcohol, it is just bad luck,

Then again, possibly not – give me a drink so I don't give a fuck.

Who or what is going to help me?

Eventually, despite my scepticism, I started to wonder if it could actually be me that was helping cause this destruction and to ask myself what I could do about it. It has been said that recovery is a selfish programme – that it is all about doing it for yourself and no one else. Still, nothing I had seen or heard convinced me even to consider sobriety, certainly not for myself.

In rehab, I was just pretending to listen, trying not to get caught looking out of the window, suppressing my yawns, not sharing with the group – in fact, I had zero interaction with anyone, to the annoyance of my fellow peers. I would agree with all the proactive suggestions made by the counsellors, and, from the realms of fantasy, I produced the most fabricated action and recovery plan imaginable to share with them in my one-to-ones.

But truth be known, I was just constantly counting down the hours to when I would have completed the treatment and could finally walk out of the door.

My treatments followed a similar pattern. The alcohol withdrawal medication always worked, with no symptoms or cravings after the first 48 hours, and I would feel cured in body and mind each time. I looked good and gave out a totally false aura of positivity, even radiance. It was very convincing (I thought). But what I was really planning to do at treatment's end was take a taxi to the local garage to buy some beers and then hurry back to the comfort of my flat for a well-deserved drink. This, to me, seemed totally normal. I even had contingency plans, giving myself at least five options to buy alcohol if anywhere was closed, and I felt no guilt or shame about this. I had done what was asked of me throughout the treatment, I was now free again, and this time I would make a concerted effort to control my drinking.

Inevitably, disaster struck. I drank more heavily. Every relapse seemed to be far worse than the one before, significantly more alarming, with even greater mental and physical destruction. I would try and drink more to drown the mental pain and to blur the physical effects, but alcohol had me in its grip again. I had no choice: another return journey back to rehab.

But, somewhere deep down, I always remembered that there was one simple consideration left to try. It had been mentioned so many times in past treatments. Through my haze of emotions in the back of that taxi, somehow I knew that there was something or someone that could help me, and this particular time I knew I had to identify what this was. Death was fast approaching, as a result of the destruction and the demonic mental and physical grip alcohol had on me.

Rehab

I might as well go to rehab to keep everyone at bay,

To prove I can stop, have the last laugh and final say,

To show that I do not need lifetime sobriety,

Leaving satisfied and confident that I can re-join a normal society.

I must admit that the initial withdrawal was terrible

But the medication in detox made me feel incredible.

This recovery program is not long, so I will play their game,

As every day I am sure will be exactly the same.

That did not take long – I am finished and once again free,

Fresh, healthy and smart for everyone to see.

Arriving home I have started drinking once again,

This time so much more intense rather than picking up now and then,

So I have to give rehab one more final go,

This time listen to everything and really take it slow.

There was something mentioned last time that I could possibly try

To open up my heart and mind for something I might identify,

But what was this? I am determined to try and find out.

Otherwise I will soon be dead without a shadow of a doubt.

What is a Higher Power?

I had decided to attend a different rehab, this time with new counsellors, peers and accommodation, so that no one could judge me and comment on my negative progress. All the same, destructive thoughts were still there within me, and now, being extremely experienced within that environment, I still just played the game.

The process was easy. First, pop high dosages of Librium (chlordiazepoxide, a benzodiazepine sedative used for short-term treatment of acute alcohol withdrawal), knowing after 48 hours of intense withdrawal, the suffering would ease, and I would feel alert, active, confident and bulletproof. Once again,

I planned and looked forward to my treatment completion and departure, with the taxi picking me up and the ritual stop at the garage for my liquid supplies. The thought was so intense that it would overwhelm me with excitement; it was like having a pint and a shot chaser in the middle of a group therapy sharing session!

In spite of my profound disengagement, however, I couldn't quite shut off totally, and something was getting through. Two words kept being repeated throughout all my treatment programmes that somehow couldn't be ignored: Higher Power. The new rehab had been effective with the detox, and I was now straight, so I listened and attempted to digest what it was all about. Was it religious? But I didn't follow a religion. Did one have to show an allegiance to someone or be part of a so-called cult? But that certainly wasn't for me. Or was it just a total sham? Then, after a lot of suspicion and doubt, I could finally visualise the concept and start to understand what this was all about.

It seemed that your personal Higher Power could be anything that you loved and had belief and faith in, so that you could establish a connection for honest communication and guidance. I was really confused and thought to myself that it must be similar to when a Catholic decides to open up in confession. I came to believe that my Higher Power could be anything – a family member, a beloved pet, or it could even be God. But how would I understand it?

It became clear that you need to have total belief, faith and trust in whatever you have chosen – three words that I now remembered, with the comfort of knowing that you can ask what you like and admit absolutely anything, good or bad. I should point out that this all took time to fall into place and took a lot of thinking through. Initially, I remember thinking to myself that this was all far too bamboozling and that I certainly didn't need to consider anything like this. Not having withdrawal symptoms any longer, I felt on top of the world, and my reward of cold beer was only days away.

It was meant to happen

I had really done it this time. On my way to my sixth rehab, I asked the taxi driver to stop at my oasis, the garage, so I could stock up with cigarettes, the only vice I was allowed. Totally obliterated, I fell out of the taxi and landed so awkwardly that I snapped my right ankle. The ambulance was called; the blue lights turned on, and I was rushed to hospital.

Upon arrival, I explained that I was a chronic alcoholic under the influence, hence experiencing no shock or pain, but that I would be in dangerous withdrawal when I became sober. The emergency staff knew full well that this scenario could be fatal so I was immediately put on a drip of chlordiazepoxide (Librium) solution.

Normally my hours, days and weeks would be identical in my periods of active alcoholism, drinking to the point of blackout. I could never remember what day of the week it was, but this time it was different. It was Christmas Eve, and my drinking was once again out of control. I was lonely, sad, angry and resentful, mainly due to having no Christmas invitations from family or friends. The A&E department was short-staffed due to the festivities, with the result that I was unable to have surgery on my ankle immediately. The effect of this was severe swelling, even with ice treatment. I couldn't be operated on until a week later, New Year's Day.

Those seven days lying in my hospital bed were the most crucial days of my life. All alone with a handful of strangers in my ward, nurses with tinsel around their necks humming Christmas carols, and with no one knowing that I was there except the rehab staff (I had asked a nurse to phone them), I realised clearly: this was insanity. Suddenly, I could now realise and understand exactly what being powerless was, after repeatedly ignoring it or pushing it aside when it was discussed in group or one-to-one sessions. Clarity came to me, and I had time to process the reality of my situation. It was not a pleasant revelation, but at this lonely and painful time, it was the most important discovery of my life and essential to my recovery. That time in hospital was literally life-saving.

On Christmas Day, there were no phone calls, cards or presents to open – not even the obligatory bunch of grapes that are always overripe. The day went so slowly, just watching waves of other people's family and friends come and go, hugging, kissing, smiling and laughing. I could see that there was empathy, love, friendship and loyalty, with an unbreakable connection of trust and honesty – and I was no part of it. I requested a doctor, lying about how much pain I was in so I could be administered extra morphine and zopiclone (a hypnotic agent used for the short-term treatment of insomnia) to put me to sleep. I'd had enough, and with tears in my eyes, I gradually nodded off.

I awoke on Boxing Day just as the sun was coming up, with everyone else still asleep and even before the nurses started their rounds. I stared at the ceiling and quietly whispered, 'My Lord, Mum and Dad, I am now ready. I want to stop drinking. Please help me.'

I had found the answer

It has been described as a miracle, and that is exactly what it was. Suddenly, I had a strong feeling of my parents' presence at my bedside and an unshakeable inner knowledge that they were there to support me. And there was another presence, much more intangible, but very strong. At that moment, I knew that I would never be alone again. Without warning, my prayer had been heard, and I was transformed. Those next five days in the hospital, I was literally floating on my bed and had nothing weighing me down. I had asked God, and my late mother and father, to help me finally stop drinking and become the son that I always should have been. Now I suddenly had immense courage, power and direction with an incredible determination to succeed. I was shaking with optimism, hope, enjoyment and enthusiasm, and the relief that suddenly took hold of me was enormous.

I can vividly remember that this incredible feeling was far greater and better than anything I had ever experienced. I couldn't wait to have that operation on my ankle, so I could hobble into rehab with a cast on my leg. This time, the difference was that I really desperately wanted to be there. Now I could honestly say that I had found, through my Higher Powers, the desire to stop drinking. I had acknowledged to them that for them to help me, I had to change. And for the first time in my life, I wanted to.

I arrived at rehab on January 2nd in the back of the hospital transport that was kindly provided. I was excited and proud to be walking through the gates a totally different person. I felt calm, confident and relaxed, holding my head up high, knowing that this time I could listen, learn and contribute. I could feel the strength and presence of my Higher Powers and that they were mentally and physically guiding me. They sustained me as I went past all my peers. They were in the courtyard on a break, inevitably staring at my plaster cast and at the hospital driver carrying my bag, until we arrived at the office for the routine check-in.

I could see someone inside moving towards the door to open it for me, so I purposely slowed down and, before I reached it, softly said the words, 'Today is the first day of the rest of my life.'

I was now ready for treatment

It was incredible that I now believed I belonged in rehab. It was time to communicate and participate, not to hide behind my mask. It was time to discard the isolation and fear that had controlled my life. But now, most importantly, I had an overwhelming sense of willingness and acceptance, which had been so alien to me and so lacking throughout my sad past existence.

The normal ritual had begun, first seeing the doctor and being prescribed Librium. This time, it wasn't a first-day formality to survive the duration of the treatment. I really wanted the medication so I would have the opportunity to apply and embrace the love, trust and direction from my Higher Powers. I knew that the withdrawal sickness would gradually diminish alongside the physical and mental pain and cravings, giving me the opportunity to start addressing my demons.

What now materialised was open-mindedness, which led me to recognise clearly who and what I actually was. This allowed me to communicate with my Higher Powers and speak with my counsellors and peers. I was now able to take advice, to accept direction and to start sharing. Finally, my willingness to confide with passion and honesty was preparing me for this extraordinary uncharted journey and showing me a totally different life.

It was then that I thought I might possibly be forgiven for being an alcoholic. However, with the association of so many character defects, and my every memory still saturated with my shortcomings, it was plain that the hard work started right now.

The excitement of starting the day

Every morning before breakfast, I would look at the day's itinerary, displayed in the dining room. I noticed that hardly anyone looked at it, or even acknowledged it was there, but I also realised that in the past I had been one of those people totally ignoring it and not accepting that it was there for a reason.

Enthusiastically reading the timetable, it was as though I was looking at a simple recipe, and with each treatment session, the ingredients for each stage would be discussed. Then, after accepting and understanding what they were, I could apply them and move on to the next stage of the recipe. This recipe is for the greatest dish ever produced – sobriety.

To put it another way, as I said above, I was on a new journey, step by step, being given the key to unlock the doors that blocked my way as I came to them so the journey could carry on successfully. One integral daily step on my way was to write a diary entry on the previous day's sessions that I had been involved in. The counsellors read this to get a true indication of how you were feeling and coping. It was imperative that you honestly wrote all your destructive and constructive thoughts, together with the emotions that had influenced your day. In the past, I would just write that I felt fine, as I knew that particular adjective would really annoy the counsellor reading it! Then I would fill the rest of the page with a detailed account of how my football team had won the night before, with endless congratulations and affirmations.

Now I wanted to recollect and express my honest thoughts and feelings so that the counsellors could see exactly the physical and mental space I was in, look at any denial, see through my mask, identify resentments and suggest boundaries. I finally allowed other people into my life. The sense of comfort and security was at times overwhelming.

So, every morning, being enthusiastic and willing, I couldn't wait to explore a different way of changing the direction of the path that I had been walking on for such a long time.

So many character defects

I had now discovered, and borne witness to, the fact that the daily recovery plan was not a chore requiring your physical and mental presence. It was there for you to start sharing and communicating with open-mindedness and honesty, to enable you to grow and develop in a joyful, creative way.

My contributions in group therapy were more constructive than I could ever have imagined. My past attitude toward this social gathering had been obliterated. I was now targeting all the character defects that had ruined my life and the lives of everyone that had come into contact with me. I was beginning to see and to understand what these were, and it became as clear as day that it was essential to recognise and to relate to all of these, right throughout my past. These defects proved to be my connection with denial and relapse and were at the root of my inability to have the desire to stop drinking.

Now I had to crush and remove these weaknesses, a daunting task but for knowing full well that I had my Higher Powers to call on for assistance.

So, as soon as I identified a defect, and the way I related to it, I would quietly sit and think about my association with it. Then, I would ask my Higher Powers to help me remove that deadly, destructive attribute. No one in the room had any idea what I was doing, of course, but I like to think there must have been a visible glow of excitement and relief surrounding me.

I could now share confidently and clearly, highlighting the shortcomings that had caused so much misery to me and to so many other people. It also became quite apparent that all these defects were exactly the same for everyone else in the room, whether they had the honesty to admit it or not.

This was the first time that, when I wrote and read out my life story again in group, it was honest. I worked hard to make it revealing, with absolutely nothing hidden or left out. I described the loneliness, torture, suffering and pain I had inflicted on myself and on others, along with the deceit, harm and inconsiderate behaviour I had imposed on all the people I loved.

So now, being in a position to see, understand and remove these defects, I was literally in a situation where I could turn the page, use a new set of pens and start writing a totally different life.

Character defects

Bite the bullet and accept humility

By surrendering to this past tarnishing inability.

It is now time to ask for that all important assistance

To change negativity with its never-ending persistence.

Look at the character defects that influence your behaviour

As these emotions are the foundation of your failure.

Find the opposite to this addictive thinking

To provide positivity and stop further sinking.

So any resentment must be turned around,

Whisper forgiveness, a quiet strength with a wonderful sound,

Try not to be angry, become relaxed and calm.

You will then find a cushion softening that unnecessary harm,

Defects and shortcomings will create a substantial list.

Each one needs to be looked at with none being missed.

All are destructive, turning into character flaws.

They need to be banished and you will be rewarded with applause.

When one is identified take time to write it down.

It must be assessed producing a smile and not a confused frown.

My way of expelling them which you will soon learn

s by asking my Higher Powers for their removal so they not dare return.

These will all finally disappear with gradual progression

As your negative emotions cannot hang on being that manipulative obsession.

Bonding and becoming part of the group

I was now committed to a programme that I looked forward to and enjoyed immensely. This involvement and participation with the honest communication it entailed, introduced me to that privileged feeling of being part of something and becoming a team member. Every member of this group had one thing in common – addiction.

It didn't matter which chemical substance was your drug of choice. The goal was identical – to be dry or clean, and sometimes both. Now, being able to partake in sessions such as meditation, acupuncture, art therapy and yoga, I started to feel a real and genuine bond with my fellow peers.

This was very obvious when we had a so-called 'feelings group' at the end of each day – a chance to discuss honestly what we were feeling. There were only peers present, no counsellors, and we could express exactly how we felt – complaints, concerns, suggestions or anything that had become irritating that could lead to resentment.

This was extremely valuable, as it allowed everyone to be laid-back and relaxed. It would have been different with a counsellor there, giving it the feel of a therapy session and perhaps waiting to pounce suddenly and analyse a slip of the tongue or the expression of some thoughtless feeling. Each night a different person would take notes so that if anything was pressing or could be potentially harmful, they could pass it on to the counsellors for them to comment on and to act on if necessary. We would always work our way around the whole group so that all had a chance to join in. Everyone was engaged, offering gratitude and affirmations to whomever we felt deserved it, and why. This could be a fellow peer, a counsellor, a particular group session or an activity – anything that you felt warranted it, due to the impression and effect it had made on you during the day. It was an excellent way of reflecting and winding down, because the emotional strain endured during rehab is inevitably severe.

Every single day was really hard work, but with each day completed, another rung on the ladder had been climbed, and you could end the day in peace, knowing you would eventually reach the top and see that elusive bright horizon that you had been desperately seeking.

There is no quick fix to rebuild trust

So, with a new understanding and direction, an empowering willingness to learn and accept help, and the recent discovery of a true bond with a new set of friends, I still had lingering, painful memories that urgently needed to be addressed.

Being saturated with the shame and guilt from my continued destructive behaviour that had spanned decades, I needed to seek forgiveness from those who had suffered as a result. This was more or less everyone I knew.

At last, it was completely clear where I had been at fault, the problems that I had caused with manipulative dishonesty and the hurt imposed on each person associated with me. These reflections deepened my insight into my behaviour and gave me the direction, determination and focus to repair the damage. In rehab, we used to compose no-send letters that were read out in group meetings, directed at friends and family, acknowledging and admitting the past with an attempt to develop the best possible relationship in the current circumstances, but to be honest, they weren't really taken seriously.

I decided how I would try to make amends to the many unfortunate people who had suffered as a direct result of my behaviour. I decided on a far less direct approach than sending a letter or arranging a meeting specifically for the purpose of making amends. Rather than a pre-arranged sit-down apologetic admittance of my faults with family and friends, I would show rather than tell them that I was sorry. This was because I knew full well what they would be thinking if we sat down together to re-hash my old shortcomings once again – that they had heard it all before, and that this chat was a waste of time. That is exactly what I would have thought if the roles were reversed.

So, I started with subtle but noticeable changes, such as not going to the bar, or mixing with my drinking buddies, and deleting their contact details from my phone. On that note, I found out when I spoke to the addicts in my group that they had done the same with their dealers. I would spend my time in AA meetings (Alcoholics Anonymous, a global fellowship whose regular meetings have helped keep millions of people sober since its founding in Akron, Ohio, USA, in June 1935). I started playing sport once again. Instead of emotional, dramatic declarations, I tried to rebuild relationships with family and friends by informal meetings in coffee shops. In these get-togethers, I would tell them that I was now starting a new way of life, and I knew that my behaviour and actions would be the only acceptable proof, and that it would take a very long time to reinstate any trust. I would be permanently making amends to my deceased parents by staying sober, but being my Higher Powers, they would be quite aware of that, anyway.

Because of willingness and honesty, the pain, shame and guilt gradually disappeared, and eventually, relationships were successfully re-established. But for me, this took years. There is no quick fix.

Trust

It has taken so long to escape addiction's bottomless pit

Totally crippling everyone associated within it.

People's wounds were deep and proving difficult to heal

As the pain and suffering that had been inflicted was just unreal.

Almighty scars then formed as a result

With any new promises ignored and taken as an insult.

The lies and dishonesty for years you have always dealt

Are lingering hurtful memories and will always be felt,

But you can push away any doubt in a gradual way

From those people lost for words and with nothing to say

By committing to a process that will make them think

That finally you have the desire not to drink.

Now changing your life in such a simple way

By practising the daily recovery plan then putting it on display,

Faith and trust are gradually starting to be built

Providing the exit for paranoia, shame and guilt.

But it will take time for this to be achieved –

Wait patiently and smile and soon you will be believed,

That you are a different person starting to prepare

For those lost relationships now determined to repair.

Most importantly you will be making amends every day

By staying sober and ensuring it most definitely stays that
way.

At night before the light goes out

I was now ready to engage in another essential requirement
for successful recovery and sobriety, and that was a nightly
review of my day.

Every night before getting into bed, I would recollect
absolutely everything I had been involved in that day. This self-
searching process is in my opinion imperative and one that will
be part of my nightly routine for the rest of my life. This, too,
was a learning process. I found I had to be totally honest with
myself while making a thoughtful review, looking to see if I had
been resentful, dishonest, selfish or scared. Did I owe anyone
an apology? Had I kept something to myself that I should have
spoken about to another person? Had I been judgemental and
inconsiderate? Was there anything that I could have done
better?

It sounds a lot to analyse just before you close your eyes,
with all the possibility of worry keeping you awake, but this

was not the case at all. The self-examination process certainly challenged me, but in a positive way, and I felt more comfortable for doing it and for facing any errors straight on. Any failures or flaws that I could highlight, I would ask my Higher Powers to remove.

My Higher Powers would never fail me, and once again, I was at peace with myself. I would sleep deeply due to my honesty and moral courage, and I would look forward to what the following day had in store. I always said to myself, 'Don't look for perfection, just progress, and take one day at a time.'

My final day of treatment

The day of my graduation had finally arrived, and my treatment had come to an end. Those last few weeks had been no mean feat; they had stretched my mental and physical boundaries to a different stratosphere, but had been the most enjoyable of my life.

I had arrived with hands up and in total surrender. My bulletproof armour and mask had been stripped from me, and was prepared and willing to engage in establishing a new direction and life. My Higher Powers had shown me a different path and had taught me how to lock the gate on the old and deadly one permanently. They had guided me and helped me navigate difficult terrain, showing me how to overcome the obstacles hidden behind every corner and turn. Suddenly the path would steepen and look like an impossible climb, but they would push, pull and sometimes carry me so I didn't give up. They were always there to help and encourage, suggesting ideas and ready with the best options and solutions. Most importantly, they would repeatedly remind me that they would always be by my side and to never forget that. I had finally reached the top of that steep, winding path, with a beautiful open plateau emerging in front of me, beckoning to be conquered. I understood that I still had a very long journey ahead, but they would always be with me to assist with every step I took.

It was a sad day leaving the rehab establishment, as I had made so many real friends there, with a bond that, in the past, would have never been able to comprehend. They were the start of a new group of people, and I longed to find more of them and to spend my time and my sobriety with them.

I ordered that taxi for a final time to take me directly home, and no stopping this time at the garage, which seemed to have disintegrated into a pile of dust. All I was thinking about was an AA meeting later that night. The excitement was overwhelming; the thought of listening to and digesting the sharing from those sober and clean people who tirelessly follow the recipe for eternal freedom. I am now able to meet them. What an honour!

All is well, right here, right now

I am now totally committed to developing a new, wonderful future with an unselfish lifestyle, full of giving and sharing. Things are looking much more upbeat and positive than I could ever have imagined.

First and foremost, I have my Higher Powers listening to me and replying to everything I ask – an inner intuition guiding me to make the right choices, and an unhesitating conviction of the next step to take. In any difficulties, whereas before I might have been confused or perplexed about what to do, the answer would just come. Not only this, but I also had the loving, considerate and trusting community in the AA fellowship. The people at the meetings were so honest and generous, it was impossible not to feel supported. They would bend over backwards to help you in any way possible. At first, I was slightly shy and reserved, especially with sharing. (AA meetings work by attendees speaking to the group about their personal story of recovery in a healthy, therapeutic way.) But, for me, it was like going to the gym for the first time. In such places, most people are immaculately toned, with a torso to die for, and as a first timer, understandably you feel uncomfortable. But your aim is to have a physique like them, which means you will have to keep coming back to the gym. This is identical to meetings – 'Keep coming back.' The more meetings I attended, the deeper my experience became. My confidence grew, and I started to feel comfortable with my surroundings and with people whose knowledge proved invaluable. The open-minded communication and sharing started to flow with an increasing feeling of acceptance and gratitude. The fellowship became 'family', giving me a gentle and loving sense of security.

The rehab held a weekly aftercare group for all those who had successfully completed treatment. It was extremely moving to see how everyone was thinking, feeling and looking, with a new glow of enthusiasm and excitement on the journey they were exploring.

At home, every night, I would write my daily inventory. I remember once enquiring of my Higher Powers whether it was right that I only seemed to have written positive feelings and actions most of the time. The instantaneous response was, 'Just wait and see.' Naturally, the inevitable did occur, and I started to recollect and to write destructive thoughts, but these defects would be removed in an instant after asking. I would also combine my daily meditation with a list of 10 things that I felt grateful for that day, slipping once again into a state of fulfilment and achievement.

I was now being given invitations from family and friends to all sorts of gatherings and events, receiving birthday, Easter and Christmas cards, even the odd present to open. But I did acknowledge that there was still a long way before their trust could be restored, and ultimately, their forgiveness gained.

This was a trail with many checkpoints, and if I reached them while implementing what I had learnt and discovered, I could move on to the next. I would find other people who I noticed were struggling on the trail, finding the bends difficult to manoeuvre or the climb too steep. I would stop and help them, show them the keys that would start unlocking the gates along the trail, and promise what would happen if they were to carry on. But, as I had found myself, the key question was: were they willing to accept this trail and the new direction in which it would lead them?

PART 2

How I stay in recovery on a daily basis

You have just read my journey to recovery. As you can see, this was hard and convoluted. The path was not straight; it took many twists and turns and was all but impossible to climb at times, except that I had the help and support of my peers and of my Higher Powers. I had no option but to share my story in this complex way so that I could fully express my confused emotional state and the consequent actions, memories and reflections. The format mirrors my emotional state of the time. This book was built on months and years of sharing and exploring with other alcoholics, friends and fellow members in AA. In this sense, I can truly say it has been years in the making. This forms the most passionate, sensitive, humble and honest personal account of my past that I have ever publicly revealed.

I have decided to write the remainder of this book in a more direct and straightforward manner so as to explain the rest of my journey more clearly and to prevent difficulty, confusion or misunderstanding with the recovery process I use to stay free from my addiction daily.

Everyone, of course, is entitled to embark on their own personal recovery programme. It depends on what you feel comfortable with and capable of achieving. You will find long-term freedom from addiction in many ways, but the actual finding of it – the admission that you cannot continue as you have been doing and that you need help – is, in my experience, the hardest part of the whole journey. So, throughout the rest of this book, I aim to share my daily recovery programme. My wholehearted commitment to this has resulted in years of sobriety and happiness. I have not the remotest desire to pick up a drink.

Daily self-care (keeping a clean house)

My process is identical for addicts as well as alcoholics, providing an emotional, mental and physical defence against cravings, triggers and relapse when you start to feel compromised – which will happen. The daily recovery process will give you an unseen, unexpected new level of energy and the opportunity to discover a whole new, pristine set of tools and to learn how to use them. It will give you the ability to stay on the new path you have just created and, using your recently acquired skills, to quickly identify and respond to any danger on that path that would inevitably lead to cracks, holes and falls.

This process can also be a code, which is a system many people like to follow and can be utilised anywhere. At the extreme end, and I hope this will never happen to you, you may find yourself in a jail cell, or you might be in a half-way house, or homeless and surviving on the street. You could be isolated due to being in a transition period, perhaps trying to find community drug and alcohol services, or finding that such projects are currently inaccessible and, in many locations, unavailable. There is always the chance that you might be trying to hide or cover up your addiction, desperate for recovery, not wanting to be exposed. So, for long-term recovery from alcoholism and addiction, here is a process that uses a straightforward set of tools and tasks as a strong foundation for recovery. This is what forms my daily self-care recovery plan. This plan is quite simply taking measures to look after my emotional, mental and physical well-being and health so I can cope with daily pressures, unexpected situations and triggers that could result in relapse. These recovery tools and tasks, which I will explain individually, have been the ongoing solution for my addiction recovery, giving me the opportunity for long-term sobriety.

A set of ingredients

Earlier on in this book, I compared our daily timetable in rehab to a recipe. I like to call my daily self-care tools a set of ingredients used to produce an outstanding, faultless dish. I look at myself as some incredible chef everyone is envious of, receiving a Michelin Star for an award-winning dish, creating a miracle that people would see, love, enjoy and talk about with astonishment as they thought such an accomplishment could never be achieved – my sobriety. But a Michelin Star, with its significance and accompanying level of recognition, has a time limit. It is not awarded for the rest of your life – it must be achieved anew, so that the highest standards are always attained. Likewise, I make sure that all the recovery self-care tools are worked and completed to the best of my ability every day so that daily sobriety is maintained and this Michelin Star is always awarded.

Like any outstanding achievement, the rewards of affirmation, admiration and respect must be worked for but are enduring. It is so satisfying and gratifying that this uncomplicated way of putting together a set of my daily self-care ingredients could destroy the doubts of the critics and sceptics, my past drinking buddies and associates, as all they wanted was for me to have a disastrous day in the kitchen!

Understandably, some people will always want to see me fail to justify their own powerlessness and total inability even to consider the slightest change to their dysfunctional, harmful lifestyle. They are constantly being marinated with denial in a simmering pot of anger, jealousy and misery – don't forget, that was once me, and perhaps you!

What I am now going to explain has been essential for my recovery, and without it I would not be sober today. Please do not skip these next few paragraphs as they are critical if you are now willing to surrender and have faith in and accept the process that I use to keep myself addiction-free every day. It is an integral part of my successful daily self-care, which is broken down further on in the book. I would sincerely like to share it with you, as I believe this is your opportunity to try and find spirituality and a Higher Power.

Desire

I had at last found that elusive desire
Not to drink again with a faith that will never tire.
With years of denial it is now time to confess
So everyone can hear my honesty to lovingly assess,
To listen and learn giving feedback myself,
Not sit on the fence or be a book left on the shelf,
Using a recovery plan that would be practised daily,
A commitment that would direct me clearly and safely.
You must complete everything and ask questions if in doubt
—
A Michelin Star dish will fail if ingredients are left out.
So now every small step will show you are willing
To embark on a future from a totally new beginning.

Spirituality

Addiction was my life, my daily existence, totally smothering me and dictating whatever I did, wherever I went, and poisoning every person I met. Finding your Higher Power may take time, but for many people, there will be that one moment when you have reached utter desperation and you cannot take any more – hitting rock bottom. I mentioned earlier in the book, in the chapter 'I had found the answer', how I had broken my ankle and was lying in a hospital bed on Christmas Day – this was that moment for me.

I was then ready to open and totally to surrender my heart and mind, allowing something else to take control of my life. This was the moment my life changed, when I was closing my eyes and begging my mother, my father and God for help, knowing I could not live like this anymore. Then suddenly the belief that they were by my side in that hospital bed materialised, astonishing as it sounds. Knowing that they were now always going to be around me took away all my fear and exchanged it for inner peace, freedom and the most inexplicable, overwhelming relief. This was my miracle and is my spirituality.

Everyone will have different views, definitions and examples of how they found spirituality, but for me it was hitting rock bottom, where I could not fall any deeper. My life had to change, or I would end it.

By immersing myself totally in my new-found faith, and trusting an entity (my Higher Powers) to provide solutions to all my problems, I discovered a spiritual miracle. This experience enabled me to explore who I was, what I wanted for myself and how I now wanted to live my life.

Spirituality for me is the belief in something beyond oneself, and if you can start with an awareness that there is something there, I believe this can soon turn into a spiritual experience. I have witnessed some agnostics or atheists starting recovery who stick with the fellowship of Alcoholics Anonymous and have found that they do gradually experience spiritual enlightenment and growth, sometimes leading to an epiphany or a moment of sudden revelation. Once you have found that imperative connection, it grows into something far bigger, greater and more powerful than you may ever have imagined.

In my opinion, religion is a way of sharing your beliefs within a group or community at various places, such as a church or a mosque. Spirituality, on the other hand, is an individual and very personal faith. Practices may not necessarily be shared and may be done on your own if you find the concept of religion an irritating obstacle. I like also to describe spirituality as a new, private way of living life that no one else knows about. It is solely about you and your connection, and so when you start your daily self-care activities, you will see that it incorporates spiritual practice. This allows you to be honest with yourself and with others, exposing where you may have gone wrong and why and, more importantly, making sure it does not happen again.

Higher Power

As you have probably gathered by now, a Higher Power is a very special, personal choice that is only known to yourself. Definitions vary, but in my view, this is an entity in which you have complete trust and faith, forming a connection that is unbreakable with its sole objective being – your recovery from addiction. You can and will find this absolute miracle if you are completely prepared to surrender to something that is far greater than you, with the ability to direct your destiny emotionally, mentally and physically.

I have noticed over the years with so many unfortunate people struggling with addiction, that when the words Higher Power are mentioned, their faces are stamped with confusion, bafflement and discomfort. Their apprehension and doubt are striking. This is then followed by a distinct air of suspicion that the whole scenario is a ploy to have them groomed or brainwashed into becoming affiliated with a religious cult or group. This also can be the case with addiction meetings and the AA fellowship, which will be discussed later. This feeling of scepticism is common. I felt the same, but after sinking to my uttermost depths of insanity, I had no choice but to reach out as I was in total desperation, not knowing what to do and whom or what to believe.

I had to find some form of private entity, something that only I knew existed – if you like, the young child's 'invisible friend' that I was able to trust, confide in and be honest with. Something incredibly special and personal to me where I could ask questions, receive answers and be given guidance. This power would never argue, criticise, tell me off or be disrespectful. Instead, it would offer me the right choices and show me different directions, guiding me along a brand-new, achievable path that I could follow and enjoy. This entity would give me the strength, courage and confidence to see and admit any fear, anger, hate, resentment and dishonesty. It would patiently listen and forgive with understanding, empathy and love, crucially never leaving my side and always being with me.

This book must outline everything connected to my successful daily recovery, so if you remember, I decided to mention that my Higher Powers were my late mother, my late father and God. I can immediately imagine the impression and defensive thoughts running through many people's minds reading this, as I have just mentioned the word 'God'. I'd like to make it plain that I am not a religious person in the slightest, nor do I have the remotest interest in the church. I have not read the Bible, and if religion is required on any paperwork, I put 'COE' (Church of England, which is just as common as my blood group, O+) as opposed to 'spirituality'. Spirituality is personal only to me, and I am not going to give any administrative pen-pusher the opportunity to judge or comment, so to avoid developing a resentment towards prying officialdom, I guard my spiritual privacy with conventional replies that don't give away too much. This is so important and is mentioned again further on in this book in the chapter 'Changing negative thinking to positive'. I choose to understand God quite simply as an entity who looks after my mother and father, but one that is far more powerful in terms of having the final say, and this belief, with its resulting connection, has never failed me.

Higher Power

For me this is my spirituality:

A sensory experience to avoid being another addiction fatality.

I had to find that entity

That would emotionally, mentally and physically control my destiny,

This would be something extremely personal and only for me,

That I could trust, confide in, and an invisible friend no one else could see.

It would never argue, criticize or have a go,

But give me guidance, direction and progression which must be slow.

This entity would create strength, courage and confidence,

Listen to any questions even if they appeared total nonsense,

Then to provide answers with a safe direction,

Never to leave my side forming a very special connection.

You will find your Higher Power when reaching rock bottom

Having no family or friends with an existence totally forgotten,

But open your heart and mind with a tear in your eye

And this entity will appear as it has heard your desperate cry,

The feeling of relief is overwhelming.

Has my addiction gone and is this the fairy-tale ending?

I am now someone that I have waited so long to be.

My Higher Power is everywhere offering a life-changing possibility.

This is not religion and is something I have never experienced or had,

So I am eternally grateful for being my miracle God, Mum and Dad.

My daily self-care activities

You might think that not drinking and going to meetings is sufficient to stay in recovery, but there is not a single person that I know, including myself, who has successfully stayed in long-term recovery by doing only this. In my opinion, daily self care activities are absolutely crucial for permanent sobriety and to prevent relapse.

Prayer and meditation

I live one day at a time and ensure that I adhere to my daily self-care programme to allow an honest, peaceful, calm and gratifying new journey. This is the lifestyle to which I have gratefully surrendered. It is imperative that you do not miss a single daily self-care activity, which can also be known as keeping a clean house, as the consequences of self-neglect can lead to relapse, if not downright tragedy. Not one activity is more important than any other, and if I might refer to my award-winning recipe, any ingredient left out will not create that daily award-winning dish!

My day starts with prayer and meditation in a relaxed, peaceful environment where I will not be disturbed. I like to call it a friendly chat where I touch base with my Higher Powers, avoiding any association with religion that might cause discomfort. It is quiet, still and tranquil, enabling you to gradually open your mind and heart for a connection with your

Higher Powers. Once this is achieved, it will totally take control of your mind and body, producing powerful, refreshing feelings of peace and safety. The more this is practised, the easier the connection will be established, especially in the early stages of recovery.

My meditation creates a comfortable, relaxed and peaceful frame of mind to create this connection with my Higher Powers. It enables me to focus my thoughts and drift into a state of open-mindedness for friendship, love, direction and strength to navigate me through another day, ensuring that I make the right choices and correct decisions. The word 'meditation', like 'prayer' used above, 'Higher Power' and many words in recovery, can have weird, tricky, awkward and sceptical connotations. I would like to stress again that, in the context of recovery, you choose the meanings of such words – perhaps even, you create the meanings as you proceed along your path of recovery. Such words are private, special to you – you do not have to borrow meanings from others. There are so many unfairly labelled stigmas in addiction, so do not let this put you off, as meditation, with practice, creates the environment to open the path for that connection.

So, first thing in the morning, I sit in my kitchen with a large cup of coffee. I do not close my eyes, which many people associate with meditation. I just gently focus on bringing the whole of my body into a state of relaxation and start opening my mind and heart, oblivious to anything else around me. Immediately I feel at ease, with a tremendous urge to reach out and share. The sense of belief and trust is so strong as I sit there, knowing that all my questions will be answered, and any lingering stress, anxiety or depression will be lovingly removed. I explain all my challenges for the day and in return am given deep, clear and meaningful alternatives on how to think and act and how to face them.

My Higher Powers help me reflect on and accept what has happened in the past with similar challenges and show me a different, positive perspective. They emphasise with clarity the different person I have now become, subtly reminding me of the past and assuring me that those defects have now been removed. There is no set amount of time that a person may spend practising daily prayer and meditation. It depends on the individual – how long does a person sit in confession with a priest? But it is essential that you stay with it until you feel you have had all your issues resolved for the day, otherwise you will be fearful and anxious of past, possibly deadly outcomes that might occur again. I'm not saying you have to clean up your entire life in one meditation session – just until your most urgent issues are addressed, and you have some practical ideas about what to do and what to let go of. With practice, you will develop a feel for when the session is 'over' – almost like a light switching off.

It is also important to note that by practising this part of daily self-care, you will find that further connections with your Higher Powers can be formed at any other time during the day to ask for further direction in situations you find difficult or that you might not have come across before. Look at certain footballers when they run onto the pitch, looking into the sky and asking for strength and direction so that they do not let anyone down. Through spirituality, your Higher Powers are always around you – they will never leave your side and will guide you at a moment's notice, steering you away from the demons that are constantly stalking and ready to pounce.

Gratitude

One feeling that typically develops after a period of sobriety, and becomes stronger with each successive day, is gratitude – starting with how grateful you are to live a life free of addiction. Every day I am cheerful, happy, joyful and accepting of myself as a worthwhile person. I did not identify these emotions at first as being gratitude – I just thought they were the initial feelings linked with my progression towards a sober future. Then, at one of my first AA meetings, another member explained that this was gratitude and that it was a fundamental element for recovery by stimulating positive emotions, and that thankfulness would reinforce a healthy outlook for long-term sobriety. So it has proved, and another self-care tool that I use is a daily gratitude list.

I always carry with me a piece of paper and pen wherever I am, or whomever I am with, and when I have the opportunity, I write down what I am grateful for. It could be gratitude for not picking up a drink, or for honesty with friends and family. It varies according to your own individual circumstances, of course. It could be having the strength to make amends to people you have hurt, or the courage to delete a dealer's mobile number from your phone. I write 10 different points every day for a week, making sure that I have not written the same one twice. Then each night I transfer that day's gratitude's onto a journal entitled 'What I Am Grateful For'. So in a week I would have recorded 70 different feelings, objects, tasks, places, situations and circumstances that I have been grateful for – the list can be staggering! Then, every week, I start again, witnessing and writing down all the good things in my life.

This recognition is a major influence on my focus and attitude and is key in preventing anything being taken for granted (or, worse, slipping into ingratitude and resentment). It promotes inner strength and resources and gives a sense of control over the many different choices that we face daily.

Changing negative thinking to positive

It would be unrealistic to expect that you don't experience any negative thoughts during the day, as they are bound to creep in at some stage even if you try your hardest to avoid them. It is so important to highlight that any negativity can lead to anxiety and stress and finally to anger and resentment – which in turn overwhelm all other emotions and increase the risk of relapse. This is the reason I mentioned resentments earlier when filling out my religion on forms. The way I combat such angry or grudging thoughts is by challenging them and, using a journal or a piece of paper, writing down a couple of words to identify the situation that brought on this negativity. Once home, and reflecting on the day, I can recall the experience and challenge that negativity, which produces surprising results.

A recent example for me is when I eagerly went to an AA meeting and on the door it stated that the meeting had been cancelled due to Covid. I felt frustrated, angry and resentful, thinking that people had not bothered to have a vaccine and so had compromised the rest of us. Immediately, my excitement and positivity sank. Shortly after arriving back home, I sat down and challenged my emotions, with a simple outcome of attending another meeting.

It was late, and with the prospect of having to use public transport, I decided to go online and watch a recording of a past AA meeting, of which there is an abundance to choose from, updated regularly. Secondly, I also reflected that the individuals involved in cancelling the meeting may in fact have been vaccinated but might have been unlucky enough to have caught the virus anyway. Thirdly, they showed their honesty in making everyone aware that they had tested positive and that any contact with people would put them at risk. So, this is my direction of thought, which worked to expel negativity and to dismantle any downward spiral that could be taking me with it.

Self-esteem

In the past, I always had a low level of self-esteem. My confidence, dignity and respect for myself were totally manipulated by the drinking. I would feel worthless and would settle for the bare minimum in whatever I did, accepting the lowest levels of achievement with no ambition or direction. These damaging, destructive and insane opinions of myself, which imprisoned me for so long in such a dark, silent existence totally influenced by my addiction, have now disappeared. This extreme level of wrongly deserved, persona (and self-inflicted) character assassination is now totally reversed in its entirety.

Self-esteem is the overall opinion of yourself, and as you progress along your new recovery path, the feeling of persona value gets stronger. It is a wonderful, positive and proud way of rewarding and motivating yourself for the milestones and triumphs achieved – and for the effort you have put in. In sobriety, we learn not to judge ourselves purely for our achievements, but for our sincere attempts, our hard work an the honesty with which we approach life.

This level of self-esteem must be honestly maintained daily as if it begins to slide, it is easy to gradually slip back in that dark place, with potentially disastrous consequences. So, during the evening, I take five minutes to reflect on the day and to write down its positive, fulfilling, and gratifying experiences by answering a set of questions that I give myself.

For example:

- Today I accomplished . . .
- I felt proud when . . .
- Something I did for someone . . .
- I had a positive experience with . . .

There are numerous different probing questions that you can find for yourself that enable you to trigger your self-worth and start to appreciate your potential. This simple daily self-care tool really works and is so important in keeping the focus on your recovery progression.

AA meetings and the fellowship

Earlier on in this book when I was explaining the various stages that enabled me to finally start recovering from my addiction, I briefly mentioned AA – Alcoholics Anonymous.

AA works by enabling alcoholics to get together and share their experiences in a therapeutic way in group meetings. The programme for this non-profit organisation is dominated by 12 key steps, which lay out a road to recovery. AA views alcoholism as an illness, and this can be a useful idea in helping people get a handle on their problem, although the disease concept has been criticised since AA's beginnings in 1935. I have my own personal opinions on this debatable theory (see the final page of this book). In early recovery it is essential that you attend as many meetings as possible, and it is a commitment that I prioritise over any of my other daily activities, such as a game of tennis or a gym session, healthy though those may be. I find that putting meetings first in this way is more important than anything else, above all in early recovery. Get to the meetings, and everything else will fall into place.

Once sober or clean, you will find it extremely easy to fit sport, hobbies and other arrangements around meetings. Addicts are usually welcome at AA meetings, although they also have their own 12-step programme, Narcotics Anonymou (NA), and if you are a recovering addict, NA will probably be your preference, but there is nothing wrong with attending both, which further on in my recovery I did. Personally, I find the main difference between the two is that AA is more focused on the help of a Higher Power for recovery and long-term sobriety, while NA has more of a focus on you as an individual, without so much emphasis on that external assistance. However, people's experiences differ, and others may find their interpretation of the meetings is different. NA does certainly allow room for a Higher Power if it is necessary to become and stay drug-free. Ultimately, it is crucial to establish what works for the individual. Both AA and NA use the 12-step programme which I will talk about a little later, but will point out now that a Higher Power is an integral, major part within the methodology of the 12-step programme and its principles.

Hopefully, there will be several locations for meetings in your area during the week. These are the foundation for sustained, long-term recovery. I attended 90 meetings in 90 days when I started my recovery journey, and you will find that this commitment is pretty much a rule of thumb and that you will hear it repeated among the people who are successfully enjoying their freedom within long-term recovery. Going to a meeting is once again on my daily self-care plan, and in early recovery, after your initial 90 meetings in 90 days, I would suggest five times a week. At one of my meetings I would make coffee or tea for everyone prior to it starting – this is called 'service' and is a great way of meeting people, but more importantly, it shows your commitment to the meeting. You will see and feel the relief and gratitude from family and friends that you have found this group of people, the fellowship, and their enthusiasm with your progression will be motivating and mentally rewarding. They have been victims for so long, a product of your addiction. As the saying goes, they will forget what you did, they will forget what you said, but they will never forget how you made them feel. Now you have the chance to make them feel differently. The way you are now living your life, for everyone, is the real victory.

Endless support

The overwhelming feelings of trust, safety and friendship are among the emotions that you will experience when first attending meetings. It can be a huge comfort to realise that everyone is the same – whoever they may be, wherever they are from or whatever they may do – everyone is held together by their common situation. It is a group of people who no longer have the desire to drink or use and who are totally focused on staying sober and clean. You will not be judged, singled out, expected to share your life story or even speak during the meeting if you would prefer only to listen. It is a group of individuals who know what it's like to be struggling with an addiction and who are now connecting with the love, understanding and support that the group offers.

These more longstanding members typically share the effect drinking and using had on them, on everyone they knew and on everything associated with them. They then explain what actions they took to stop the catastrophic destruction and how they moved on to their lives of daily freedom. You will find that in their past there was a great deal of failure and despair that you can probably relate to, but I have also found it is truly refreshing and uplifting to witness the hope and strength of these people. Their contribution really helps generate that one, mutual desire to recover and stay recovered. I do not think you can start recovery by trying to do it all by yourself. Addiction is too powerful – you will give up, you will relapse, you will fail. So do reach out for the support that is all around you at meetings.

In particular, the more experienced members sometimes take individual newcomers under their wing, acting as what are called 'sponsors'. Sponsors offer support, a friendly ear and sometimes a friendly warning – for they can be as alert as counsellors for any self-deception or weaknesses that might lead the way back to a drink. They will guide you through the working of the steps and generally support your personal development and spiritual growth. There is no formal arrangement – if you do not get on as well as you hoped with one sponsor, you are free to change to another, and different sponsors may be relevant at different times of your recovery as you grow and change, although you should beware of chopping and changing too much. It pays to take your time and look around before first approaching someone to see if they will be your sponsor.

Good boundaries are important. There is an unwritten rule that a sponsor should not be someone of the opposite sex or, in these days of more fluid gender definitions, someone with whom there is a risk of getting romantically involved. (This risk in the fellowship is well known as the 13th step.) Although you can expect to share honestly with your sponsor, remember that you are likely to be vulnerable in early sobriety, and do not ling yourself into a sponsee relationship with the first likely person you meet. Test the water, get to know the person, attend lots of meetings and ask around. Do not take on anyone whom you feel dubious about. And if a sponsor or potential sponsor makes you feel uncomfortable, or judged, you are free to walk away and to reconsider, and be reassured, no offence is ever taken. There are people of all kinds in AA, so take your time until you find someone who is a good fit for you.

Remember, you are never alone in AA, and the meetings are there to help you recover and keep yourself in recovery. Do not get put off by any naive, false images of the group – that it is a cult, sect or movement, for example, and it is certainly not political or religious.

There are guidelines called 'traditions' that provide a successful structure for the meeting, with a set of promises that outline your destiny by accepting, working and completing the 12 steps. This destiny is of course freedom. Depending on your time of sobriety, you will receive 'chips', which I like to call medals, recognising your incredible, miraculous achievement of being alcohol or drug free – whether it is 24 hours or multiple years, it boosts self-esteem to new heights. You will feel so proud with the recognition and affirmation from the warmth of the group – you really will feel that, no matter how harrowing your past, you have become a worthwhile person.

AA and the fellowship

This is an amazing group of people who have the ability

To immediately offer safety, love and stability.

They will open their arms on your arrival

As their only concern is your survival.

Every single person has one thing in common –

A desire not to drink again, which was always the problem.

They will share experiences throughout a meeting

To prove you are not the only one who took a beating,

A group of individuals getting together with addiction to blame

From all walks of life and exactly the same.

The kindness and time these people set aside

Is overwhelming to you and is impossible to hide.

Now appearing is a new family and a different set of friends

That will patiently listen and show you how to make amends.

Within this group a particular person you will find

These are called sponsors – no charge but all out of kind,

And will try and help you with everything you need to know

Due to your mind being made up and ready to go.

They will introduce the 12-step program when your commitment is fine,

A set of principles for long-term sobriety but still one day at a time.

AA and the fellowship are not religious or a cult,

No sect or movement and certainly not political as that would be an insult.

It is spiritual – that may take time to grasp and embrace

But recovery is a progression and not a race.

Finally, do not miss a meeting and start to become slack –

AA and the fellowship are the solution, so keep coming back!

The 12 steps

The 12-step programme is a set of principles that will assist anyone who is in addiction recovery. It is an integral part of my recovery and many others', and its colossal success is a testament to its effectiveness. It crucially builds and develops the strong structure needed for long-term addiction recovery. In an earlier chapter, 'Endless support', I mentioned the importance of a sponsor. One of the sponsor's roles is to help take you through the 12 steps of the programme. The steps require you to take various measures and respond to them for successful long-term recovery.

For example, the first step asks that you make a simple declaration of powerlessness over alcohol. This in itself is an immense relief for many people as they realise they can give up the battle they have likely been waging for many years. It certainly was for me. As I stated earlier in this book, this acceptance of powerlessness was the turning point for me as I realised on that hospital bed that my life truly was unmanageable. This is why I chose the title of this book – *Surrender* really says it all. Surrender is absolutely key to sobriety and a calm, contented, successful life.

Surrender is not the end, however – it is very much a beginning. An admission of personal powerlessness paves the way to receiving the help and support that are so desperately needed. But more than that, it also opens the door to working the rest of the steps and to a whole new life. AA has various 'promises' that will occur if the work on the steps is done and constantly practised – freedom and happiness, being able to forget the past and having a new and powerful intuition on how to handle problems that may previously have overwhelmed us.

The other steps focus on handing over our problems to a power greater than ourselves – the Higher Power I have been talking about – whether that be the group or a spiritual entity, or both. They also present a way to come to terms with the past by self-examination, making amends and service – which again I have outlined. All in all, they form a practical and spiritual package to work your way through at your own pace on your road to sobriety.

Sponsors will explain this process to help you understand the principles and how they may apply to you, offering guidance and constant encouragement as the steps were not meant to be taken on by yourself. I would speak or see in person my sponsor several times a week, and this would not only help me but also them to deepen their knowledge, experience and commitment by constantly helping others who are so vulnerable in early recovery.

The 12 steps

For me and so many these steps are an essential guide

To overcome addiction and help if you begin to slide,

And at last giving you belief and hope

So you can finally climb off that slippery slope.

They are principles and a methodology

If you are prepared to participate with total honesty,

It will look at your past and provide a new future

Absolutely imperative if you are an alcoholic or a user,

Giving you freedom if you change your behaviour.

But only if you work these steps will they become your saviour,

And after working these twelve steps

A change you will see within your character defects,

Proving to you that if you surrender

Long-term sobriety is achievable and certainly not slender,

Finding that new courage and hidden strength

By facing present and future fears at extraordinary length.

You will be granted an elusive integrity

Appearing from a moral foundation influenced by sincerity,

To change your life which is so fulfilling,

There will be no hesitation if you have faith and are willing,

Holding your hands up and accepting humility,

Something that has always been a non-existent ability,

Leaving you embraced with affection and love,

Driven by spirituality and your Higher Powers floating above.

The steps provide a new responsibility

For motivation and destroying any volatility,

Showing you boundaries that require commitment and discipline,

Armoury you have now generated and improving daily from within.

The direction of the steps will provide so much awareness,

The only way of recovery which is my opinion in all fairness

When ready, reach out to try and help others,

The ones that struggle with acceptance which addiction smothers.

Tell them to remove that mask as there is no need to hide

These are the twelve steps to freedom, the most perfect guide.

Daily reflections

So, the day is nearly ending and you have willingly worked through all the daily self-care tools with faith and honesty, managing successfully to live another amazing day in recovery – but it has not finished yet. I mentioned earlier in the book how I made a final connection with my Higher Powers each evening, to reflect on the day before going to sleep. This proved one of the keys to my initial recovery, and I find it is essential to carry this on every night to help maintain long-term daily freedom from your addiction. Being night, it is a calm, peaceful and silent place, and sitting on the side of the bed I form that connection once again.

There will always be something irritating and worrying you that has happened during the day that you cannot stop thinking about, and this needs to be identified so you can ask your Higher Powers for clarity and a solution, otherwise you may have a restless night. I search back through the day to see if I owe anyone an apology for being self-centred or self-seeking. Was there a situation or a confrontation where I felt fear, anger or jealousy that would lead to resentment? Absolutely anything may surface, no matter how small, trivial or irrelevant it may seem – it will be answered. In this time of calm reflection, you will be shown a different, clearer, more understandable view of that niggling emotion, along with a different direction to take should the same obstacles appear again. But it could also be the case that your day has just been a total pleasure, and all you are itching to say is how much gratitude you have, expressing this to your Higher Powers for that final chat of the day. So as you can see, by working all the daily self-care tools to the best of your ability, you are now ready, once again, for a wonderful night's sleep.

Aftercare

As you have read, I was lucky enough to be admitted into a residential rehab for my alcoholism treatment, and part of the establishment's aftercare service was to provide a weekly aftercare group to discuss progress and air any problems. This facility is normally offered in any addiction treatment centre. I attend every Saturday, again arranging any commitments around that two-hour group so that it is prioritised – nothing gets in the way of my Saturdays. It is a source of strength to return to that room, in that familiar, safe and comfortable environment, sitting next to my old peers. We share our experiences since completing treatment, and at what stage we are at in our recovery journeys, as no one is the same – I have already said that how you stay in recovery is an individual choice on as long as it works. We spend this valuable time giving feedback on issues such as triggers, relapse prevention and rebuilding relationships, discussing our own personal coping methods and the ways in which we are making amends. This meeting is also very beneficial in terms of gaining experience and confidence in listening and sharing, to help practise for the AA or NA meetings you will be attending during the week.

Rehabs

This brings me nicely onto the subject of rehabs, whether residential or outpatient (you do not stay there overnight). It is my opinion that if you have no intention of becoming sober or clean and you have already decided that you will pick up a drink or use again, then rehab is a total waste of everyone's time, effort and money. Using the establishment to repair a relationship, to obtain early release from jail or to prove to yourself and other people that you can abstain from substances for a brief period is ludicrous. Anyone with the right medication can do that. Your mindset will still be the same, in that you think you can control your drinking or using and lead a normal life like everyone else. WELL, YOU CAN'T. My late father spent thousands of pounds financing my treatment. These payments were written into a black book so that later, when his inheritance was shared between myself, my brothers and my sisters, they all received a cash lump sum; I was given an invoice! It does not matter if you go to the most expensive rehab facility on the planet – money will not buy you sobriety. Every time I picked up, my relapse was far greater than the last time, and the more intense were the consequences, eventually opening the door to suicidal thinking. For treatment to be successful – and by that I mean long-term, not just a flash in the pan – you must make the choice not to drink or use drugs ever again. I did, and if I did it, then anyone can!

If you are not able to attend a residential facility due to circumstances such as finance or location, then an outpatient addiction treatment centre should be available. It will provide during the day the same services as residential rehab – the initial detox platform, then recovery treatment, concluding with the formation of your personal self-care plan to keep you drug and alcohol free. Some of these you have to pay for, but there are establishments that are government funded, and indeed I have been to one.

There are a few countries in the world where a person's medical insurance will cover the cost of staying at an addiction recovery treatment centre. Too often, all this does is provide an opportunity to have a short period of time alcohol or drug free under a supervised detox, and then a four week 'jolly'. Therefore, these establishments are frequently like a conveyer belt, with the same people constantly going in and coming out with very little intention to stop picking up or using. These treatment centres must be highly profitable. In the last issue, it is your choice to stop drinking or taking drugs, but the key thing is your inner attitude. If there is the slightest feeling of surrender to treatment, if deep down you really have had enough, but you just do not know how to address or deal with it – then there is hope, and one of these centres could be the answer.

Treatment, like mine, will address the fundamental causes of your addiction and will outline coping mechanisms to overcome these for the future. This is another ingredient for success – it doesn't just address the physical mechanisms of drinking or drugging, but what lies beneath them. This process will also help you assemble your own set of ingredients for another award-winning Michelin Star dish!

There are alternatives to 12-step programmes, such as Smart Recovery, and I have read that this views addiction as a bad habit that can be changed. As I understand it, spirituality, Higher Power and the 12 steps do not feature at all, and an individual should become self-reliant in order to maintain sobriety. Smart Recovery involves cognitive behavioural therapy (CBT), which is an evidence-based type of talk therapy with a strong scientific foundation. I cannot comment further as I have never met anyone who has committed to this recovery treatment.

Triggers and boundaries

Throughout your day, addiction will be waiting, watching and monitoring every single situation, location, movement and environment you are in. It is easily remembered by using three words – people, places and things (association). Addiction will stalk you, masterminding a tug of war with your emotions and thoughts, one side wanting sobriety and the other to pick up or use. It will try and manipulate, control and influence your actions, and it will put into motion a sequence of thoughts to justify another drink or drug. Addiction is subtle and convincing, and unless you prepare yourself, you risk being caught in its trap and becoming a prisoner once more. These addictive thoughts and feelings are called triggers and are basically anything that you associate with having a drink or taking a drug. They might be any one thing from spending time with people you used to meet drinking, to visiting places with negative associations or simply looking at a credit card as a chopping tool if you are an addict. For example, one trigger for me was the garage!

Usually, triggers are obvious enough to be identified, assessed and avoided so that the consequence of relapse is evaded as best you can. You could even compare it to dodging a bullet. It is not about making the decision that you will not pick up a drink or use a drug that is important – it is making the decision not to expose yourself to a trigger that is the most important.

On the day I left my final treatment centre – and this could also have been a prison cell, half-way house, hospital or detox unit – I compiled a list of people, places and things that always led me to a drink. Your reflections must be honest, with no debate. Dismiss at once any whisper of temptation – 'I might have had a drink in that situation' or 'I wouldn't have thought I would use with those people in that environment'. This is your addiction talking. It's all about putting the work into your recovery, and if you start trying to hide vulnerability at this early and critical stage, it unfortunately proves that you are still in denial, trying to find opportunities to carry on drinking or using. I am not implying that your life and existence should be one of a recluse or hermit and that you cannot meet people, go anywhere, or do anything. It is just a list to remind you of the past with its devastating consequences if such factors are not approached properly.

Before I accepted that I was in denial, the only boundaries I knew were the ones connected with cricket. But boundaries are critical, lines you do not cross, as if these are crossed again another relapse is highly likely. So boundaries must be though through in depth and need to be precise and clear but also achievable. Boundaries are generally the same with everyone that has experienced addiction. Some are obvious, like social events, pubs, bars, restaurants, clubs and concerts. Possibly you might set a boundary on some of these events as being just too high risk for you to attend, or you must leave at a certain time or not go anywhere near your old 'friends', the barflies. There will always be birthdays and funerals, financial success and bankruptcy, marriage and then a massive chance of divorce, all providing yet another chance to drink or use, especially if your life has been governed by addiction. Everything is fuelled by emotional, mental and physical responses, but by committing to the daily self-care programme and using its simple recovery tools, you have a tremendous chance of not being compromised. Again, I cannot emphasise more the importance of practising each recovery step.

This is a good opportunity briefly to mention something else. For me, there is an irony about Alcoholics Anonymous in that I do not wish to be anonymous. I am so proud of achieving daily sobriety that I would like everyone to know that I was a chronic alcoholic! In the past, I have had a drink of zero-alcohol lager, and the question that always prevailed was, why was I drinking that? I would then explain the reason, which became the centre of conversation, which in turn formed an excellent way of reflecting on my past, especially with those people who are not, or choose not to be, aware of the seriousness of the illness. Some people reading this will think that having a drink like this is an outrageous risk, so why have I even mentioned it? Even alcohol-free beer can be a serious trigger for some, and many people choose not to sample any form of alcohol-free beer, wine or spirits throughout their recovery. I would have to agree – but my book must be totally honest, with absolutely nothing left out. So, a huge red alert warning – a scenario like this in early recovery, while of value to me personally in spreading the message and hopefully helping others, might very well enhance the chances of relapse due to the temptation, association and cravings, so please do not try this! I do not wish your recovery to be compromised.

Triggers

Triggers will be by your side for the rest of your life

Hiding everywhere to ambush and cut you down with a knife.

Addiction is so cunning it will patiently wait

After watching you and discreetly placing the bait,

Hoping a situation or event will make you collapse

With a temptation or sudden urge that would lead to relapse.

But just reflect and identify where in the past you had gone wrong.

Make an honest list spotting which occasion all your money had gone.

It could be a variety of celebrations,

Or a tragedy where you offered sincere commiserations.

What about that unexpected promotion

That led you to being drunk, producing so much staff commotion?

Avoidance is imperative in early recovery

So aim for sobriety, a wonderful discovery.

You do not have to be a hermit or a recluse,

Now being sober and a different person, just put it to good use.

But be wary of what you do and where you go.

As with any relapse, the whole world will eventually know.

Meet up with people as you are gratefully not under addiction's spell

But set yourself a time limit with an imaginary bell.

It is a boundary you keep and have made your call.

Cinderella did the same at that magnificent ball.

Dealing with relationships

My main trigger to this day is relationships. I have always picked up to absorb, mask and temporarily smother emotional grief and sorrow while wallowing in self-pity after a break-up. There was a phrase that I read that is so relevant to alcoholics: 'Under a skirt there is always a slip.' Today this sounds rather sexist, of course, but the point is that romantic relationships entail a particular kind of vulnerability. In any case I assure you that I state it with all due humility and from a rather painful wealth of experience! I found that I had to set a boundary when I first started recovery, so I did not have (or was not able to have) a traditional relationship at that stage. Instead, I had to opt for one that had no commitment or allegiance and where I did not have to be accountable for anything. However, I still longed for romance, excitement, lust and sex. I found this by joining the swinger community, which offers an alternative relationship direction. Swinging is basically an open relationship. 'The Lifestyle', as it's called, is a consensual sexual arrangement where liberated singles, couples or married individuals meet up, swap partners and have sex. After talking to many non-monogamous married couples, they have confirmed that this novelty in the bedroom has increased the attraction between them, extended their relationship and, for some, ultimately saved their marriage. More importantly, the deterioration of the relationship in one of the couples had been a direct result of past addiction issues.

With singles like myself, finding a partner or a couple for the evening vastly improved my self-esteem. I was once again desired, bringing back that feeling of being a worthwhile person. These arrangements are normally NSA – No Strings Attached – which means there is no commitment after you have been swinging together and no further interactions unless mutually arranged. There is also FWB – Friends With Benefits – where an agreement could be made to swing together on a regular basis, again without making any commitment or forming a relationship.

On the internet, there are many types of websites offering lifestyle alternatives – but be careful if you decide to try them out. Apart from the general need to keep safe online, you could start messaging someone who has been computer-generated, so ultimately sharing intimate desires with a robot! The two I use and would recommend are AFF – AdultFriendFinder – that has an enormous number of like-minded adults throughout the world, which is very useful when you are on holiday – and a more local site that primarily offers swinging contacts in the UK, aptly named Fab Swingers. Here is where you could find a possible match in the most remote of places and rural hamlets, which is not surprising as the swinging community is growing at a phenomenal rate. Both sites provide information on swinger clubs and parties, which again are everywhere and offer a wide range spectrum of swinger dynamics, depending on one's curiosity or possibly courage to experiment.

I regularly visit a swinger club in Nottingham, England called Purple Mamba, which deserves a mention as it was the first club I went to and which helped significantly with my confidence and forgotten basic social skills. But, essentially with me, it created a safe place to enjoy the night, with no paranoia, anxiety or feelings of worthlessness. I was truly welcomed, without being judged – I have to say this with a smile on my face – just like an AA meeting!

I apologise if this sounds slightly detached, but with my history, I simply could not afford to get involved in any form of relationship – it was literally a matter of life or death for me. Anything that sent me towards a drink, however remotely, had to be avoided at all costs. If swinging does not appeal to you, or is not possible due to where you live, then I encourage you to think about other ways in which you can get these very natural needs met. Discuss it with your sponsor and your Higher Power, and with a therapist if need be. Make a list of your needs and your relationship issues, trusting that they will be met in time – then hand the list over to your Higher Power. Put it in a box for six months or a year and look at it then – you may be surprised. Some people opt for a period of abstinence from relationships while they grow the strength to handle them; others test their emotional muscles on more neutral relationships like friendships, associations with other AA members and work relationships where the boundaries may be more obvious. Once these are in place and working well, it can then be easier to move on to more challenging romantic relationships. We are all different, however – the main point is to be aware of how relationships affect you.

Addiction is so clever that it knows that relationships are my main trigger, and any form of connection, in any scenario, with a female is still an opportunity for it to work its claws into the depths of my mind. I get so fed up, as it creates relentless, intolerable anxiety and paranoia with tiny, unimportant things assuming huge significance, such as not answering texts immediately or cancelling a meeting (hook-up) at the last minute. Addiction creates turmoil within my thoughts and starts to conjure up the most ridiculous reasons and conclusions as to why this has happened. Unreasonable as it may seem to outsiders, this anxiety is so relevant in these situations, as anxiety is a direct result of wanting to control any future outcomes, which I have to admit is certainly the case with me. Due to this addiction-related turmoil, I then feel compelled to try and express these feelings to a partner, even though I know they are totally unjustified, and I come across as an over-possessive thorn in her side. Understandably, she then tends to withdraw and to start to create distance between us – who can blame her, as it's not what she wanted, and she certainly is not answerable to my anxiety and qualms.

I have seen these kinds of emotional responses within relationships in many people. It is common, especially with the growing burden of anxiety in our society, but the difference with alcoholics and addicts is that the impact is far greater and potentially life-threatening. I know many sober people who, like me, have had to make the decision to withdraw from relationships for the time being as they were unable to control their emotions. I would say that this knowledge, and acting on it, denotes insight and inner strength. In the last issue, it protects others as well as the individual concerned. Only with the help of my daily recovery tools and the faith I have in my Higher Powers to provide answers did I once again have the desire not to drink in such emotional contexts, but it will take a little bit more time yet for me to become stronger and finally to control these emotions. So just be aware, addiction is working all the time and will never take a day off.

Dealing with relationships

You could find it so hard to control your emotion.

Even in successful recovery it provides devastating commotion.

Trying so hard to fight back the anxiety

As this could be the end of your hard-fought sobriety.

The paranoia and stress are so intense

And with an excellent daily recovery plan it just does not make sense.

But you are still clingy and unfairly possessive,

As the war inside your head fuelled by jealousy becomes aggressive.

These voices of addiction will not give in,

Only your Higher Powers will stop you from throwing recovery in the bin.

You are always being sceptical and convinced everything is lies,

Which of course is totally wrong and that is no surprise.

Worthlessness and inadequacy crash your self-esteem.

These demons have risen with a strength never seen.

So to stop all this I have found another way

To still show my character and true self and putting it on display.

This is why I am a swinger, a no-strings attached arrangement

Enjoying private meets with no commitment marriage or even an engagement.

Everyone knows exactly where they stand,

Visiting clubs and parties which have a real potential to expand.

This scenario is definitely right for me,

So if you are curious try it and you will soon see.

It has taken away my main trigger to stop me from relapsing.

And there are many experienced people willing to keep me practising.

Comparing yourself to others

There are going to be a few people reading this book who are still in denial, seeking an avenue for self-justification to carry on drinking or taking drugs. You may be using this literature purely for the purposes of comparison, to see if you are or were as 'bad' as I was, and if this is the reason, you may make an instant judgement that none of this applies to you. But if you have even picked up this book and have been reading up to now, the chances are that you know you have issues. If you are being honest with yourself, it's likely that will be shame, guilt, dishonesty and lies, and you are desperate to find a compromise where everyone wins. You have an addiction where no one wins. THERE IS NO COMPROMISE.

Someone might have asked you to read this book or similar literature, and I can honestly say that my late father would have done just that. He did not know what to do or say, confused and desperate, watching his son whom he had meticulously brought up with so much love, affection, devotion and protection being crippled with alcoholism, each day adding more nails to the coffin.

All I am saying is that everyone around you can see your issues; they are only trying to help. They only want you to get better by finally accepting your addiction and surrendering to your denial.

It is so common to compare yourself with others; this was my justification to carry on drinking for years. I would see and feel the incredible torture to which people had subjected their family and friends, shattering love, relationships and any trust that they tried so hard to keep. I would listen to horrific life stories that were absolutely devastating, bringing tears to everyone's eyes. I would look at the physical disabilities, some severe, that were a result of their long-term addictions. I would process everything so defensively that everything would appear far worse than what I had done or what I had put people through. And believe it or not, I found this reassuring. You must understand, as I eventually did, that there will be different life experiences – family wealth, residential location, upbringing, education, employment, social status and your circle of friends. But the result is identical, with the drinker or addict inflicting the same agonising misery, pain, hurt and distress on everyone around them. The solution is simple. All people want is for you to admit that you are extremely ill, totally powerless over your addiction. Then you can take action to get better.

Deflection

You will also become an expert at deflecting any probing from others. Any questions directed at you, any queries about your life – these can all be turned back onto the questioner. You tend to be very good at evading the intrusion, dismissing any such enquiries. Your self-taught fine art of diversion swing into action and takes control as you throw yourself into their concerns or into other people's problems. This is all done by showing understanding, compassion and empathy and then outlining practical solutions or a different way forward, whether you have been asked for this or not. It is a deceitful and fraudulent masquerade that is a defence mechanism that addiction has taught you, producing a robust and convincing mask to hide behind. The more you practise and progress with the daily self-care programme, though, the more this mask wi slip and your true self will come out of the shadows and start t shine brightly.

Complacency

On many occasions before I eventually relapsed, I was not thinking about picking up a drink in the slightest, but I had become complacent, cocky and smug. My over-confidence, and more importantly my self-satisfied attitude, led me to believe that I had nailed recovery and that it was literally a wa in the park. My sobriety was progressing nicely, thank you, an was being rewarded with endless affirmation, admiration and applause from every direction. I could not put a foot wrong – I was again bulletproof. This, as I have just mentioned, happened several times throughout my past turbulent attempts at long-term recovery, convincing myself once more that this time would be different. When you ignore any warning signs, relapse is imminent.

The three stages of a relapse – emotional, mental and physical

1 – Emotional relapse

Addiction is a genius, knowing full well how to start covertly disabling the foundations of the fortress you had so willingly built for yourself. The emotions form a vital part of this structure, and emotional sobriety is at the root of physical sobriety. So if you are 'feeling off', take it seriously before it can morph into anything more. I found I had to be alert to any slippage in my feelings, and it is interesting that my emotions would start to slip and deteriorate in an all too predictable fashion well before I had any overt thought of a drink.

First, my general commitment would slip – I would 'bend the routine', start procrastinating and putting off practising the essential daily recovery tools. All the dedication and priorities I had worked so hard to establish started slipping away, then totally vanished. When I did eventually try to catch up and start resuming work on my recovery, due to the ever-persistent niggling, shame and guilt, my efforts were rushed and slipshod, with no real thought, meaning or purpose. The connection that enabled all my daily chats (prayers) with my Higher Powers, my meditation and reflections had become inconsistent, unimportant and brief. I was once again losing confidence, self-esteem and faith along with my identity, and when I attended AA meetings, I would purposely arrive at the meeting late and leave early, and I certainly would not share. Whenever I met up with family or friends, my emotions were tightly 'bottled up', being replaced with extravagant ambition and unrealistic, fabricated personal goals.

Then isolation started gradually to take over. In fact, I would deliberately isolate, taking the easy, comforting option of staying home to avoid socialising, and the days I would phone into work sick rocketed, with eventual, inevitable consequences. There were no more training sessions at the gym, or releasing my well-earned abundance of energy on the tennis court. My daily personal hygiene started to become a chore, and my normal healthy appetite for nutritious food disappeared.

If my mobile phone rang, I would just stare at it until the call went dead, leading to unjustified resentment and twisted, insane thoughts of people trying to intrude into my life. Sleeping became erratic, so I was always tired, irritable and angry, resulting in extreme negative thinking and a feeling of being unhealthy, dirty and once again worthless.

For some reason I did not ever get depressed, but the formidable strength of this hostile direction of thought did lead to paranoia, anxiety, stress, pain and fear. The permanent struggle with my emotions introduced crippling doubts and fears that I was not capable of recovery and that my life was far more enjoyable when I was drinking. I knew full well that I had to speak with someone – anyone – but my mind just refused. So as you can see, with emotional relapse, tension builds up with your thought patterns and actions, setting you up for failure.

2 – Mental relapse

The mental turmoil and confusion that invaded my mind during these periods created an intense battle, with one army wanting to stop drinking (or using), and the other, addiction, looking to pick up and have one (or a few). There is so much strength within both opposing armies, and a compromise will always be used to establish the outcome. Compromise is the perfect weapon for addiction – by spotting and focusing on this weakness, it can see and feel your mental retreat and then start to utilise all its resources to exploit your damaged defences. So, beware compromise – it never works for the addicted person.

Addiction will lead its final advance in several different directions, by targeting and influencing everything you do, and as many successful clever strategies. In this war of attrition, addiction is an intelligent enemy that will grind your mental defences down and over time will force you into submission, making you physically pick up that drink or use that drug.

My cravings for a drink would start to creep in and then to snowball as every day passed with any resistance hopelessly melting, until the intense desire became overwhelming. I just could not stop my direction of thought, insanely convincing myself yet again that I had finally arrived at a stage where I could control my drinking, and that it would definitely be different this time. Shame and guilt would never give up, still trying to battle and heroically act as my last line of defence. These emotions would fight so hard to keep my mental thoughts and actions sane, by reflecting on my past and remembering once again the agonising disappointment, sadness, sorrow and unhappiness that would always follow m succumbing to alcohol, where everyone watched me deteriorate and slip back into the tight grip of addiction.

The next level of this downward spiral is inevitable, and if unlucky enough to get caught up in it, most of you will start meticulously to plan when and where to pick up that drink or use that drug. The feeling of worthlessness appears yet again even more overwhelming than before, and coupled with the shame, guilt and remorse, it creates massive paranoia. Your mental creativity is triggered and works overtime to ensure that no one will suspect that you have failed miserably at another attempt at a life of sobriety.

But the devious and brilliant plans must be better than last time, or your relapse will be easily spotted. One of my favourites was always a change of location, and I would regularly catch a train or bus to a different town or city, spending the day in the closest bar or pub to the station. Then of course there were the periodic relapses with those unsuccessful holidays abroad – yet surely this particular trip would be different, and when arriving back home you would stop drinking without hesitation.

In times of relapse, you tend to find that suddenly your enjoyment comes from the excitement and challenge of where and when to pick up that drink or to use that drug without being caught. All your mental energy is now totally focused on the kitchen wall calendar where you have written your forthcoming social events. These could be invitations from family and friends showing trust and respect for what they think is a fantastic achievement, sobriety – trusting people who sadly have no idea what your real intentions are right now. Not only will you be a cheat, a liar and a fraud, but you may well feel that your selfish, inconsiderate and hurtful intentions are worse than any atrocity or crime, with no regard for your family and friends and no consideration for the renewed faith in you that they painfully spent so long rebuilding. You may well be facing the prospect of everyone's work – yours as well as theirs – going down the drain, and risking the prospect of them throwing you back among the dregs of society once again.

Remorse and alarm may have little effect on you, however. Instead, what can be called alcoholic cunning accelerates – the ability strategically and logistically to plan the opportunities to find, hide and then pick up that drink. All this tends to become paramount, excluding other types of thinking. In addition, you may find yourself masterminding exceptional exit plans and escape routes that the most prolific bullion thief would be proud of, while mentally rehearsing various scenarios of being caught and concocting genius excuses and alibis. Your justification and reasons are word perfect, no stage fright, with an award-winning script worthy of film director Walter Hill.

Now your mindset, mood, morale and mental condition are irreversible, being totally overrun by a joyous anticipation of picking up again. But, insanely, you may still think that your drinking is controllable and that you can work, socialise and live a normal life while harbouring a secret that even Agatha Christie's Miss Marple cannot figure out.

Addiction has once again infested, corrupted and saturated your being. It has taken over, tearing apart the hard-fought final defences you worked so hard to build up and allowing cravings to become ferocious and uncontrollable.

So, from having the strongest and most invincible desire not to drink, things have radically and drastically changed to having an uncontrollable and unmanageable desire to pick up or use once again. The gate on that path that you had worked so hard to climb is now closed, and the majestic, sunny, bright horizon has totally disappeared. All those people you once so proudly walked besides – nowhere to be seen. Addiction promised you that it would be different this time, with a compromise being possible, and that you would be the first person to walk this planet who would be able to make the choice whether to have a drink or not. Addiction granted you the ability to decide when to stop if you chose. Fake promises. This new, attractive path suddenly becomes all too familiar, except that it is far darker, more isolated and more miserable than the last time you walked it, with the fear and pain rapidly becoming intolerable. Your shame and guilt reach a new intensity, far worse than ever before, strangling your self-esteem and destroying your character. The feeling of failure not only tortures your emotions but fuels the demands of a worthless identity that you have managed to assume yet again. Addiction's seduction has had its reward.

3 – Physical relapse

You have just reached stage three of relapse – physically picking up a drink or using a drug. I am not going to write a lengthy, painful explanation on this stage as there is little to say about an accomplished fact. You can be pretty sure that the drinking or using has inflicted another wave of extreme distress upon yourself and everyone around you, with a corresponding progression of emotional and mental turmoil. You are back in that room of broken promises, with no light, no windows and not even a door. It is isolated, dark, silent and terrifying, with just enough space to bury your face in your numb and shaking hands. Cries for help go unheard, and any communication seems impossible; you have returned to imprisonment, courtesy of addiction. But there is an extremely important twist to this custodial verdict – as the length of the sentence is entirely up to you.

Relapse is an opportunity

The feelings of worthlessness, failure and anger sink to new depths. Once again, you have been deceived, beaten, consequently losing all your respect, dignity and pride. Shame and guilt inevitably create severe paranoia and relentlessly revolving anxiety, and you may tear yourself apart with obsessive fears of what family and friends must think of you.

Please do not forget that their opinion has no value at all unless you decide to give it any. I was told in many therapy sessions that it is about accepting that you can totally blow something, without it having to describe, define or categorise you.

There could be several reasons why you have relapsed. First it is probably worth reflecting on the people, places and things you have been around (association) and also going through your trigger checklist. There will likely be a tremendous number of excuses, which is quite normal for a person who sti wants to drink or use. At first, I found it extremely difficult to imagine a life without alcohol, with all the fun suddenly disappearing, and this was one factor that scared me back into drinking (to no avail, I might add). Another time, I was influenced by fear and anger stemming from the thought that I could not ever recover in the first place, as I was so scared that I would turn into someone that I, and everyone around me, would not like.

This especially applied to relationships, as alcohol supplied the confidence to produce spark, wit, subtle sexual innuendos, quelling any attraction – a lethal cocktail that I always thought worked. These relationships always started and ended in bars. Scenarios like this convinced me that I could drink on certain occasions, with the belief that I could control my alcoholism and get the best of both worlds, especially after various decent lengths of sobriety. Inevitably, on every occasion I left myself totally exposed to the wrecking ball that would appear from nowhere (as it seemed), smashing any pride, dignity and sanity to pieces. This produced so much turmoil and negativity that it crippled my self-confidence, self-respect and self-worth and destroyed my honour and morale. From this, I would conclude that recovery was too difficult and that I would never be able to achieve it. As previously mentioned, I used to compare myself to other people, concluding that my addiction was no way as severe as theirs. Ring a bell?

These excuses are not worth the paper they are written on. They just create muddled thinking. The key thing to bear in mind is that recovery is possible. No matter how many times you may have relapsed, it is always possible to have another go. Do not listen to addiction's chatter, either to its beguiling false promises or the barrage of remorse and 'beating yourself up' that may follow a slip. Just pick yourself up and start again – you can do this.

But first, some clear thinking. If you honestly have the desire to recover, you must see these excuses for what they are and acknowledge that they are a part of addiction's armoury, specifically designed to create negativity by penetrating and destroying any positivity. So now we can start all over again, but this time with more humility, accepting what has happened and learning from it. Start focusing on positivity and composure, creating willingness, strength and courage and erasing any negative thought activity for a final time. There is nothing to be ashamed of with a relapse if you are prepared to open your mind and heart and have faith and trust to a process to which you now finally surrender – a process that will lead to a life of joy, harmony and real, long-term sobriety.

Look at why you stopped working your daily recovery. Was it because you were HALT? – an acronym I learnt in rehab, meaning Hungry, Angry, Lonely, Tired. This combination can be a huge sign of trouble.

All is not lost. Relapse provides a chance to work on your underlying resilience, to build up your strength again from within and to attack any final remaining areas of weakness. Look on it as a process, rather than one mighty task that must e achieved all in one go. Remember to take it one day at a time and to ask for strength on a daily basis.

So, make a decision to put the lapse behind you. This is your opportunity to push the refresh or reset button or to give your safety valve, your daily self-care activities, a full service, so that the next time the drink or drug tries to worm its way back into our thoughts or is staring you in the face, you have the coping ools and strength to say no.

Reassess your boundaries and triggers to avoid those high-isk, compromising situations and temptations that may nfluence you so that the chances of any further possible elapses are now minimal. You will probably feel ncomfortable in such situations, having made the decision ot to drink or use, but you will get used to that feeling – it oes gradually disappear, and eventually you will feel totally omfortable in situations where alcohol is present. Stick with , and far enough along the line, you won't even give it a econd thought.

Daily self-care I personally think is sometimes not given the redit of being the most important part of anyone's day-by-ay recovery. It is for me, and I hope you can now see that it ill be for you, too, as it has all the tools to utilise on an ngoing basis. Also, when meeting, listening and learning from thers in recovery, try absorbing their different ways of eflection, communication, sobriety methods and direction. ut do not forget your daily self-care, enabling your best chance of success with long-term sobriety and keeping that really clean house.

It is now down to you

I sincerely hope you have enjoyed reading my ongoing recovery journey. Hopefully, you can now see a straightforward way that will help you recover and stay recovered from addiction – but only if you surrender, have fait and trust in everything required within the process. Please, do not try and take shortcuts or bend this process – it will not work, and you will fail once again.

I had to change my life, and so will you; there are so many people in early recovery who think that change is not necessary and that they can stay as they are – this is wishing for a relapse. You do not have to change everything, nor do you have to change all at once, but you must change your boundaries and be aware of those triggers, red alert areas tha come from those three crucial words – people, places, things (association).

Any negativity, with time, will instinctively be turned into positivity, and your confidence with talking and sharing will grow. You will be able to ask questions, process the answers and never again be afraid to ask for help. This is why AA, the fellowship and your sponsor are so important. Everyone is in the same position, having faced the same dilemmas, problem and challenges, overcoming bumps and cracks in their recovery paths and gratefully sharing these experiences for others to learn from or relate to. This is a group of loving, caring people who will honestly explain any misunderstanding, confusion or delusions you may have so that you become a part of a family striving for permanent freedom, from the minute you have the courage to step through that door.

If you feel that your emotions are suddenly starting to play tricks and games, this being the first of the three stages (emotional, mental, and physical) that lead to relapse – have no hesitation in crying out for help. We have all been there, bottling it up and putting on that mask while deflecting any concerns or just staying quiet. You must not forget that 'Silence has the loudest voice'.

Honesty is imperative throughout your journey. At first, this may seem odd or can be a struggle as addiction requires lying, and we all had become exceptionally good at it. (All politicians surely cannot be victims of addiction!) Honesty is a bit like riding a bike – it can take time to acquire the skill, but once you do, it never really leaves you, no matter what lies addiction continues to whisper in your ear. Be honest about what is wrong with yourself and not what is wrong with other people, and try to take that step to be honest all the time. This could prove to be difficult and uncomfortable – it certainly did for me – but with practice and time it tends to become much easier, and at times you may even find that you end up laughing at yourself. Another essential, for me and for many others, is gratitude. This is an integral part of overall happiness and joy. Developing positive feelings is not only motivating in itself, but essential for personal daily growth. A good way to grow gratitude is by focussing on it in your daily reflections.

Finally, open your heart and mind to find, understand and experience spirituality. Build faith that enables you to discover your Higher Power or Powers that can assist in every part of your journey to freedom, happiness and long-term sobriety. So, thank you, God, Mum and Dad, I am so grateful and love you so much – I'll catch up with you later!

It is now down to you

You have now reached the end of my book.

I am so grateful you decided to take a look!

There is absolutely no way of conquering addiction.

If in disagreement you are following a dream of total fiction

Addiction will affect every generation to come.

If there were a prescription remedy it would have already been done.

Alcohol and drugs will be available 24 hours a day

So this is something I really have to say.

It is controversial but don't ignore the truth –

I know some will argue until they are long in the tooth.

Alcohol is a social part of everyday society

For those fortunate folk who have no need for sobriety.

The drug cartels spotted a business opportunity,

A profitable enterprise that the whole world could see,

It is a very straightforward supply and demand

That through expansion they totally and fully command,

With faultless logistics and international supply.

Delivery is impeccable on which they rely,

It makes you wonder and seriously think

Those famous online companies copied this strategy so they didn't initially sink.

But addiction might be defeated with my solution

Rather than waiting for Armageddon or Earth's destruction from pollution.

It is admitting that you are out of control,

Fed up with your existence and life as a whole,

Being influenced and manipulated with everything you do

Like a puppet on a string or a caged animal in a zoo.

Your existence disappears, finally coming to a halt

No one believing that it is not your fault,

But not having any idea what to actually do

After finally deciding a new life is definitely for you.

If you surrender, a miracle will materialise,

Something just incredible taking you by surprise,

It is having the faith in Spirituality,

So not to become another addiction fatality.

This entity will eventually occur

Being crystal clear and not a blur.

You have now opened your heart and mind

Through shear desperation from a life so confined.

At last you are willing to accept anything

To conquer addiction and the freedom it will bring.

You have found that imperative connection

That will embrace you with loving kindness and protection

And you will need this every single day

As this cunning enemy addiction will never go away.

This Higher Power will give you direction

To take the right path in case you make the wrong selection

Making sure your daily recovery plan is always done,

Giving praise for another successful 24-hour battle won.

You have to realise the recovery tools are essential

To reveal that person inside you with so much potential.

You will relish every day and it will not become a chore

While ignoring sceptics who have now become such a bore,

With faith trust and honesty you will go so far,

Showing everyone what a worthwhile person you are.

Recovery is not quick, it is about progression

It was not long ago you were crippled with that obsession.

So gradually develop and watch yourself grow

Slowly stepping forward and letting the past go.

Enjoy the fellowship with everything it brings

And keep talking about those irritating, awkward things.

This is your chance now knowing what to do

To repair an unfortunate past that you totally blew.

An alcohol and drug free life is definitely not too hard.

Follow my simple recovery plan but always be on guard.

One day it will be your turn to give and offer assistance

As cries for help are permanently in the distance.

So now I am done and it is up to you

To start a life which is totally brand new.

Finally there is just one thing that must not be missed,

And that will be putting me on your very first gratitude list

A final comment for what it's worth

I personally think that alcohol and drug addiction is a menta health issue and needs to be addressed accordingly.

There will always be the debate about whether it should be classified as a disease, due to chemical substances altering the brain and causing it to function differently – the foundation of addictive behaviour. But I strongly believe that it is a mental obsession, an obsessive-compulsive disorder creating an overpowering desire for more, leading to an individual becoming physically dependent on alcohol or drugs.

Surely the way forward is to treat a person's mind and thought process? People have found a warm and comforting paradise when drinking or using, covering up, blanking out an temporarily eradicating the issues of daily life. But these issue often gradually increase covertly in severity, so that those affected are hardly aware of it, and they have their roots in past traumatic, unforgettable experiences and afflictions. No amount of alcohol or drugs will eradicate such memories. It is the same as applying a band aid to a cut – it is a temporary solution, but this particular cut will never stop bleeding.

Dame Carol Black was appointed to review the UK government's drug policies in 2019. Her final report revealed in February 2022 that underfunded treatment and recovery services increased drug use and increased harms from drug use, leaving these services on their knees. The financial cost of this drug misuse was estimated at a staggering 20 billion a year. Dame Carol Black's report recommended substantial increases in funding and support for individuals with substance misuse problems.

In line with Dame Carol Black's recommendations and their 2021 drug strategy, the government in 2022 introduced a 10-year strategy, From Harm to Hope, acknowledging that substance misuse is not just a law enforcement issue but a problem for all of society. Primarily, the aim is to give serial offenders the chance to get off drugs and turn their lives around, providing comprehensive education in schools to stop young people being dragged into a life of drugs and crime.

Their investment is three billion, and in their words, the ambition is to bring hope to those who have long since lost it and to help rebuild lives so as to bring about change, which the government admits is so badly needed. The plan represents a welcome move from criminalising addiction to viewing it as a chronic health condition that needs quality treatment.

It is imperative that far more free walk-in facilities and government-funded residential and day addiction treatment centres be made available for people so that they have the opportunity to attend group therapy meetings, to talk to others and to speak out about their concerns. To give them just a tiny ounce of hope and direction so that they don't feel ostracized and forgotten. To help people identify and work out their underlying issues before they give up through frustration and take the easy route of the insidious solace of drinking or using – a 'solution' that is affecting thousands on a daily basis.

Alongside this, our society must constantly be made aware of and reminded of the consequences of chemical addiction in their entirety – to be shown the effects that will result if people persist in abusing substances. We need to take alcohol and drugs education to a whole new level. There need to be public broadcasts on television; literature should be made widely available, dropped through people's letter boxes and placed in prison cells and probation offices to educate people about the devastating effects substance abuse has on family, friends, employment, finances, housing and, most importantly, health, with a worldwide fatality rate ever increasing.

Money needs to be spent on national campaigns, especially to target the younger generation by introducing alcohol alongside the current, very basic, drug awareness as well as sex education in all schools, so at least they have a chance to realise the resulting effect of addiction at a young age. This kind of education would have to take on the 'laddish' culture s prevalent in many schools, where drinking is seen as a kind of rite of passage to cool and successful adulthood, and where easy access to drugs is becoming an increasing problem in teenagers and even in younger children.

For the unrealistic optimist who thinks the legalisation of drugs could be the solution, pull your woolly head in – this will never happen, in my opinion. Even if it were to take place, just to provide a hypothetical answer, it would only produce a massive increase in casual usage, which would inevitably lead to further abuse and dependence. A surge in hospitalisation would take place, with a huge financial burden for the public health service, and the costs to this and to economically dependent workers would make a mockery of the financial benefits of legalisation.

Addiction is not a legal problem that costs billions worldwide in law enforcement and a relentless revolving incarceration cycle – it is a public health issue, and this has to be the new approach. The so-called war on drugs has proven to be totally ineffective, and any further money made available to combat drugs can be spent far more beneficially.

Addiction will never stop in our society, but it can be slowed down. A new culture must be established that accepts the demonised stigma of addiction, allowing people not to be afraid to come forward and talk about their problem, to feel safe and comfortable, knowing they won't be intimidated or scrutinised. It is so important, and this is why I repeat it, to start integrating addiction education into schools to give the next generation a chance to say no rather than being swallowed up by an ever increasing epidemic of drug and alcohol abuse. Currently too many young people are influenced by gang culture, and if anyone disagrees with me, then they really have serious everyday society awareness issues!

Finally, we need to give more help to the unfortunate individuals who are unable to escape the justice system, as they haven't been shown a way of stopping their addiction that they can understand, trust and have faith in. We also need to increase opportunities for them to carry on with their recovery in an aftercare service after their sentence has finished. In the past, I have been a volunteer looking after prisoners who have just been released, and they are often totally lost. They must be given direction on how to change their lives, otherwise they will endlessly re-offend, resulting in a huge daily expenditure for the taxpayer.

Surely the maths must prove that a change is needed, and I sincerely hope that the recent funding is properly utilised, showing commitment and the understanding of a severe problem. Let us hope that the government's 10-year plan does bring about results with the financial assistance not being cut; unfortunately, from what I've seen, the majority of our society wouldn't bat an eyelid if this were the case.

Having said all this, I would not want to end on a down note so I would just like to add that I was delighted to read of

Catherine Middleton's personal appeal to alcoholics and drug addicts to come forward for help. The princess of Wales, patron of the Forward Trust, whose mission is to empower people to break the cycle of crime and addiction, urged people not to suffer in silence through shame or fear, but to seek help. Her words launched the charity's Taking Action on Addiction campaign, 2022. Recovery is possible, stressed the princess – and with this thought, I leave you.

I would be so grateful if you could write a review on the Amazon product information page for "SURRENDER".

The section can be quite tricky to find but please do not give up; I certainly didn't with my faith in addiction recovery to achieve long term sobriety.

@longtermsobriety

117

Printed in Great Britain
by Amazon